52 THINGS
SONS NEED
FROM THEIR
DADS

JAY PAYLEITNER

HARVEST HOUSE PUBLISHERS
EUGENE, OREGON

Cover by Left Coast Design, Portland, Oregon

Cover photo © auremar / Shutterstock

Jay Payleitner is represented by MacGregor Literary Inc. of Hillsboro, Oregon.

52 THINGS SONS NEED FROM THEIR DADS
Copyright © 2014 by Jay Payleitner
Published by Harvest House Publishers
Eugene, Oregon 97402
www.harvesthousepublishers.com

Library of Congress Cataloging-in-Publication Data
  Payleitner, Jay K.
  52 things sons need from their dads / Jay Payleitner.
    pages cm
  ISBN 978-0-7369-5780-9 (pbk.)
  ISBN 978-0-7369-5781-6 (eBook)
  1. Fathers and sons—Religious aspects—Christianity. I. Title. II. Title: Fifty-two things sons need from their dads.
  BV4529.17.P395 2014
  248.8'421—dc23

                                                    2013030808

        14 15 16 17 18 19 20 21 22 / BP-CD / 10 9 8 7 6 5 4 3 2 1

What People Are Saying About
52 Things Sons Need from Their Dads

"Is there anything a man will ever do that is more daunting and rewarding than investing in his son? Jay gives us both inspiration and practical pathways so a dad can reach out to his boy and say to him with passion and conviction, '*Follow me as I follow Christ.*'"

—**Brian Doyle,** founder and president of Iron Sharpens Iron

"You can do this stuff!...Jay Payleitner shows you practical ways to be a better dad in the little things now—so you won't have regrets later. I love this book."

—**Tim Shoemaker,** speaker and author of *Super Husband, Super Dad* and
You Can Be the Hero Your Family Needs

"Jay's new book continues to give parents wisdom and insight into healthy relationships—this time the unique and powerful bond between a father and his son. If you want a close relationship with your boy, I recommend you read this book."

—**Rick Johnson,** bestselling author of *Better Dads, Stronger Sons* and
A Man in the Making: Strategies to Help Your Son Succeed in Life

"Every son longs for the affirmation and blessing of his father. This book is a great practical tool to help complete that transaction. These 52 things are a great investment for any father to give his son."

—**Dr. Jim McBride,** executive pastor of Sherwood Baptist Church
and executive producer of Sherwood Pictures

"Readers are inspired and entertained by Jay's positive, thoughtful, and funloving ways. With warmth and respect for his family, Jay takes his responsibility as a dad seriously...without taking himself too seriously."

—**Ellen Banks Elwell,** author of *The One Year Devotions for Moms* and *Life Is Beautiful*

"Reading Jay's engaging book...took me back to my youth working side by side with my dad on our farm. I learned about love, hard work, and leadership. The same kind of lessons all dads need to pass on to their boys."

—**Bob Tiede,** director of Global Operations Leadership Development for Cru
(formerly Campus Crusade for Christ)

"The most important thing a dad can give to his son is his time. In these 52 easy-to-read chapters, Jay gives you plenty of ways to make that time meaningful."

—**Tom Cheshire,** lead servant, Relevant Practical Ministry for Men

"Dad: you're the best person in this world to disciple your son…And Jay shows you 52 ways to do it without your son's even knowing it, using the real-life opportunities you already share."

—**Leary Gates,** venture catalyst, speaker, author,
and president of the National Coalition of Ministries to Men

"Candid insights and practical wisdom for any dad entrusted by God to help forge the next generation of men. If you have sons, you won't want to miss out on Jay's powerful and easy-to apply ideas."

—**Karol Ladd,** bestselling author of *The Power of a Positive Mom*

"Jay understands that being a good dad is about the everyday 'stuff.' The ideas and challenges here will help you raise your son to stand strong and secure in the love of his earthly father—and his heavenly One."

—**Carey Casey,** CEO of the National Center for Fathering, radio host of *Today's Father,* speaker, and author of *Championship Fathering*

To the finest four men I know.
Alec Jay, Randall Jay, Maximilian Jay, and Isaac Jay.

Acknowledgments

First, of course, to our heavenly Father. Above all.

Then, I must credit most of the dads I know for doing an extraordinary job. This world desperately needs the next generation of men to wield great character, wisdom, and integrity. Thanks to any man committed to getting his son ready for battle.

A few courageous friends even helped shape the content of this book. Thanks to Jerry Jenkins, who issued a challenging foreword. Plus Dan Balow, Dave George, Dick Graff, Jim Nicodem, Dennis O'Malley, Tim Hollinger, Terry Schweizer, Glen West, and Ron Preston.

Other dads of sons who contributed more indirectly are Mitch Belon, Josh McDowell, Jack Hibbard, Jack Goldthwaite, Tim Shoemaker, Phred Hollister, T.D. Decker, Joe Priola, Gary LaGesse, Dan Stellato, Warren Beeh, Larry Stratton, Tim Sjostrom, Steve Clausen, Andy Doyle, and Eric Rojas. Thanks also to the leadership teams at Iron Sharpens Iron, Man in the Mirror, and the National Coalition of Ministries to Men.

Rooting specifically for this project were Carey Casey and Brock Griffin at the National Center for Fathering, as well as Terry Glaspey, Paul Gossard, Bob Hawkins Jr., and the entire gifted team at Harvest House Publishers.

I'm very grateful to the pastors and event planners who have invited me to encourage, laugh with, and challenge diverse throngs of dads and husbands. It's always fun and always rewarding.

Love and thanks to my bride, Rita. Life with you gets impossibly better every year. I am inspired and humbled just thinking of my daughter, Rae Anne, and my daughters-in-law, Rachel, Lindsay, Megan, and Kaitlin.

To my first grandchild, Jackson David Payleitner. Wow.

And, finally to my four sons—Alec, Randall, Max, and Isaac—who every day prove that fatherhood is a blessing beyond anything I could imagine or deserve.

Contents

Foreword
by Jerry Jenkins

One of the oldest clichés is that kids don't come with instruction manuals. So what do we parents do? We go looking for one.

If only we could find some Dr. Spock or Dr. Dobson or Dr. Phil with a short list of keys, rules, handy shortcuts. Just give me the steps I need to follow to raise a son...

Has my friend Jay Payleitner done that? Has he distilled parenting sons into 52 bullet points?

You might be wincing, wishing the list were shorter still..."Yet if you're telling me that if I can accomplish these..."

Meanwhile, Jay and I are chuckling. We've been there. We know the truth. He's raised four. I've raised three. And the fact is, there is no blueprint. There are no shortcuts. We hope you've picked up this book because you're eager for all the help you can get.

And while there is no magic formula, you have come to the right place for come-alongside expert help from someone who learned early the all-in, 24/7 (if I may employ the second-oldest cliché) nature of the parenting task.

For years dads have scoured the landscape for easier ways to manage this assignment. The old quality time vs. quantity time gambit sounded attractive. It went like this: if you don't have a lot of time to spend with your boys, make sure the time you *do* spend with them is...wait for it (add a drumroll if you can)...*quality time.*

In other words, don't just sit around playing games or watching TV. Discuss—what, let's see—the meaning of the cosmos?

If I've learned anything from my three sons it's that they hear what you say, but they believe what you do. You tell them they are your top priority. You prove that with love. And love is spelled T-I-M-E. Quantities of time.

I agreed on a policy with my wife even before our first came along, and that was that I would do no work from the office and no writing from the time I got home from work until the time the kids went to bed. That gave me several hours a day devoted to them alone.

This was not necessarily structured time. We could talk. We could sit. We could play. They could climb me. Ignore me. Whatever they wanted. Putting them to bed every night, teaching them Bible verses, singing with them, praying with them, and hearing each of them put their faith in Christ are treasures I would trade for nothing on earth.

As my sons grew up they naturally grew more independent, and we didn't always agree on everything. But they did not rebel, and they were never disrespectful. Neither did they ever doubt my motives. My devotion to them convinced them of my love, and they are my best friends to this day.

Something else to be aware of: parenting never ends. Our eldest two, who are married and have kids, have both recently added more children via adoption. I could not be more proud. Our youngest, who had a brush with death before our eyes after a routine operation (he's back to full health), reminded us that regardless of their age, your kids are always your children.

So—sorry, it's not easy, and it never ends. But nothing else you ever do will be as rewarding.

You'll discover rich benefits in Jay's 52 suggestions, and I pray that before you reach the end, you will begin adding at least 52 more of your own.

—*Jerry Jenkins*
Jerry B. Jenkins is a novelist and biographer
whose more than 180 books have sold over
70 million copies.

The Father–Son Staredown

When you look at him, you see yourself. But in raw form.

When he looks at you—if he's around kindergarten age—he sees a hero.

To maintain that title, all you have to do is show up and follow your instincts. Goof with him. Toss him around. Play Rock/Scissors/Paper. Read picture books. Marvel with him about bugs, dandelions, and shiny rocks. Get down on his level and really talk to him. *Shazam!* You're an instant superhero. I recommend you bask in that title as long as possible.

As he approaches the teenage years, some of that is going to change. A maturing son should look at his father and still see a hero. But now in human form. Blue jeans instead of tights. Car keys instead of telekinesis. A steady income instead of superhuman strength.

You're still a champion of sorts, but your relationship shifts from fiction to fact. You offer stability. You're a reliable resource, someone he can trust.

To keep that hero status, you need to be honest, respectful, and even vulnerable.

Your teenage son's admiration for you has nothing to do with your being invincible. You're a hero every time you listen, show appreciation, exhibit patience, solve problems, overcome challenges, and even admit when you don't have all the answers. The result is a relationship built on shared consideration. You respect him. He respects you.

Too many parents buy into the myth that raising boys is one frustrating confrontation after another. Some look at a teenage boy and see nothing but trouble waiting to happen. Don't believe that lie.

Next time your son enters the room, don't say a word. Just look at him. Notice his slight swagger. His clear, curious eyes. His mischievous smile. His jawline. His strong shoulders. If you don't see it all, that's okay. It'll come.

Keep your eyes steady until he says, "Whatcha lookin' at?" Then respond, "You. Just thinking about how awesome you are. Wondering what your life is going to be like in ten years. I'm looking forward to it."

I don't know how your son will respond. My four sons, who are all out of college, would probably shake their heads and say something like, "Crazy old man." And they wouldn't be wrong.

My friend, I implore you to enjoy every minute of the great father–son staredown. Don't blink. It'll be over before you know it.

A Son Needs His Dad…

To Be a Student of His Growing Son

For the first few years of his life, you know all the things he knows. And he knows you know.

You are his world. When you play "peek-a-boo," you are teaching him that Daddy might leave for a certain length of time, but he will always come back.

When he starts to crawl, you put a stuffed doggy just out of his reach. He scoots after it and you pull it farther away. He scoots again and you pull it farther. That's not mean. (Unless you never let him catch it.) You're teaching him tenacity. When he finally grabs it after three (or four) times, he learns the value of perseverance.

You are right there to watch his face light up the first time he has a taste of ice cream. You roll a ball to him and his reflexes evoke the poise of a major-league shortstop. He stares at a goldfish or studies a trail of ants on the sidewalk. When he looks up with that wonderful wide-eyed expression of new discovery, you share the moment.

When you play "guess which hand" or hide-and-seek you are teaching him about spatial relationships and body awareness. When you sit together and watch a sunrise or you point out constellations in the night sky, you are helping him discover an order to the universe that didn't happen by accident.

That's why quantity time is so important. It builds security in you. It builds security in him. You feel some control. You feel like you can stay a step ahead of your son. Every discovery he makes is one you have already made. When he shares a new insight with you, you are making lifelong connections. He runs to bring you a shiny rock or a dirty penny and you reward him with an "ooh" and an "aah." He hears a boom of thunder or a tire squeal, but it's not scary because he looks up and you're not far away.

Safe and secure is a good feeling. It's a result of shared knowledge and shared experience.

Even when your little guy spends a day at Grandma's, the security is still there. If your son tastes grapefruit or sees an opossum for the first time, she's going to tell you about it. For a finite length of time, you have a firm handle on who he is and everything he knows.

And then suddenly you don't.

Your son's acquisition of knowledge—without Mom or Dad around—begins in earnest when he goes off to preschool or kindergarten. Then it accelerates through elementary school. He spends hours every day learning things that you can't possibly know about. Some of it is taught to him quite intentionally in textbooks and lesson plans. As much as you would like them to, teachers, coaches, and other parents won't run their worldview or life philosophies past you for your approval before presenting them to your son. Other kids bring all kinds of information and misinformation into your son's world.

Scary? Yes. But don't give up now.

For one thing, you need to remind yourself regularly that the goal is for junior to eventually head out on his own and learn things you can't possibly teach him. All his knowledge and skill building should *not* come from you. Yes, you're awesome. But don't you want your son to be even awesomer?

At the same time, you also need to remind yourself that he still has a dozen more years under your care. But instead of being his sole teacher, your role has expanded. You have begun the season of fatherhood in which you are also a student of your son. Your in-depth study includes noticing and evaluating his gifts and talents. His struggles and shortcomings. His goals and fears. What excites him or frustrates him, and how he interacts with others.

Much of this is simply observation. So you'll want to continue to enter his world as often as possible. Visiting classrooms, coaching his teams, volunteering at church, leading a scout troop, playing street football with his buddies, and shopping for blue jeans and school supplies. Invite him into your world as well. Let him know about a challenging project you're facing at work, walk together down the aisles of Home Depot looking for the right door hinge or can of spray paint, take him to the driving range, or sign up for a father–son shift at a soup kitchen or shelter.

With intentionality, study your growing son. You'll know when to challenge him and when to back off. You'll know when the time is right to place new opportunities in front of him that may lead to self-discovery and growth.

You'll know when to push him to the edge of his comfort zone and beyond. You'll know when to rescue him so he can try something else. You'll know when to let him fail so he discovers that he can survive setbacks. And maybe even learn from them.

Years from now when you're no longer right beside him, he'll still hear your voice encouraging him to move forward with courage and conviction.

═══════════════════════ **TAKEAWAY** ═══════════════════════

Your son may very well follow your exact career path. Someday you may even paint the words "And Son" on the side of your delivery van. That would be so cool. But chances are your gifted son will pursue a career that you can't even imagine. Still, you can take some of the credit. Because you were the one who challenged him to extend his vision, try new things, and pursue God's very best call on his life.

"Too many parents make life hard for their children
by trying, too zealously, to make it easy for them."
—JOHANN WOLFGANG VON GOETHE (1759–1832)

A Son Needs His Dad...

To Not Kill the Creepy Centipede Right Away

Our first house had a minor bug infestation. Creepy crawlies commonly referred to as centipedes. One day—instead of smashing one of the fast-moving bugs—I trapped the critter under a clear water glass. As Rita cringed, I called my preschool-age son, Alec, over and told him I had captured a centipede, and then asked him if had any ideas on how it got such a silly-sounding name. The discussion unleashed a barrage of knowledge acquisition both entomological and etymological. With a dash of math thrown in.

Entomology, of course, came in as Alec and I attempted to decide whether or not the creature was an insect. This was before the Internet, so we only had my limited biological training to guide us. I recalled that insects have three body parts and six legs, so this definitely did not qualify. Spiders have eight legs. Worms have no legs. In the end, we decided it was probably tasty to birds, but had no other use except for the pleasure that comes from squashing it.

Of greater interest was the name itself. The etymologist in me came out and I told Alec how words can often be broken down in parts. *Centi + pede.* I reminded him that there are 100 cents in a dollar and 100 years in a century. Also, you pedal a bike with your feet and people who walk down the street are called pedestrians. So centipede means "100 feet." Alec thought that was a pretty good name. We could have expanded the lesson to talk about how the octopus got its name or what happens when Mom goes for a pedicure, but we saved that for another day.

That investment of a few minutes and a dash of creative brainpower yielded a little science, a little English, a little math, and one young curious mind made even curiouser. (Remember now, all the while Rita is on the other side of the kitchen saying, "Just kill it." Which we did. With a satisfying crunch.)

That in a nutshell is a pretty good example of the difference between a mom and a dad. Around the house, Mom has a list of things that need to get done—in the next decade, later this year, later this week, later today, or immediately. She's got a family to run and only so many hours in the day. There's just no time to get sidetracked by identifying bugs, counting legs, or discerning the Latin derivation of a word that sends shivers down her spine.

But Dad has a perspective that sees into the future. Dads do things moms typically don't. Catching bugs, snakes, and chipmunks. Counting the rings in tree stumps. Pausing a leaf-raking project to consider the reason geese fly south in a V-formation. Waking kids to see a lunar eclipse at 2 a.m. Slowing down at a construction site to note the different types of Caterpillar earthmovers: backhoes that scoop, front loaders that lift, bulldozers that push.

Moms want sons to fold their napkins in their laps at dinner. Dads want sons to get their hands dirty, create mild explosions, climb to the next branch, and somersault down sand dunes.

When she looks at a growing son, Mom envisions a charming daughter-in-law and a few grandkids, and she hopes he makes his home not too far from home. Dads see a future career in biology, engineering, horticulture, literature, law, medicine, or big business. He may also see a son destined for the NBA, PGA tour, or Olympic gold. (Don't push too hard there, Dad.)

All of the above, obviously, is why God designed families with a mom and a dad to balance priorities and possibilities in the life of a growing boy. So yes, eventually you do need to honor Mom's request and squash the centipede. Don't forget to clean up the bug-goo residue. And then, Dad, look for the next exciting, unforgettable teachable moment.

TAKEAWAY

Take the lead in establishing your son's worldview. In those serendipitous moments of life, sprinkle in truths about how the universe was formed by a Creator God who loves us and how we can live by standards of right and wrong. Conversely, moral relativism suggests that there are no absolute truths or moral standards, so any law can be passed for any reason. If that's the case, the bug-protection police could break down your door and arrest you for squashing the centipede. And who wants that?

> *"A single swallow, it is said, devours ten millions of insects every year. The supplying of these insects I take to be a signal instance of the Creator's bounty in providing for the lives of His creatures."*
>
> —HENRY WARD BEECHER (1813–1887)

A Son Needs His Dad…

To Know He Is Not a Clone

It took a while, but I finally came to realize my four sons are not my clones. I have my strengths and weaknesses. They have theirs. Of course, there's some overlap. But when I think of their accomplishments and convictions, I am proud to say each of them are far better human beings than their old man will ever be.

This chapter will serve as an introduction to those boys and a confession from me. From oldest to youngest, allow me to list four real-life examples of specific things they have done that I would never do.

Alec spent almost a decade as the front man for a working rock band. Maybe you were one of the many fans of "Fool's Crow" in Champaign-Urbana or "The Bandages" in Chicago. I still have many of their original songs running through my mind. I cherish the evenings spent watching Alec and his bandmates perform. No way could I have done that.

After Randall graduated with a double major from the University of Illinois, he planned an extended trip to Europe with some pals. The plan was for Randall and Jake to spend a week in Ireland and meet up with Stephen later in Italy. A couple days before the trip, Jake came down with meningitis. My 22-year-old son took his knapsack and slept in hostels and cheap motels exploring Ireland on his own. Kind of romantic, but not something I would have ever done.

Junior year of high school, Max blew out his knee in football, had surgery, and was told that involvement with winter sports was out of the question, but with intense therapy he might be healthy for the spring baseball season. He wrote five words on a sheet of paper and stuck it to his bedroom wall: "JANUARY 18—GET IT DONE." Max attacked rehab with that goal. Beginning January 12, he won 14 straight wrestling matches to earn a conference championship, regional championship, and a trip to the state finals. By comparison, my senior year of high school, I jammed a knuckle on my left hand and sat out wrestling for two weeks.

Without any previous exposure to farming, Isaac graduated with a degree in financial planning from the University of Illinois's famed agricultural department. Then he took a great job 150 miles from home. I know nothing about farming and have never lived more than 10 miles from where I was born.

That's just a quick flyby of some of the ways Alec, Randall, Max, and Isaac are way different than me. Again, that's a good thing. And it's proof that Rita and I have given them enough room and courage to make their own decisions along the way. As they grew, each of them knew we were always there with a listening ear, regular words of encouragement, occasional words of caution, and specific advice when asked. They also knew we were praying for them earnestly and regularly.

Of course, we weren't sure where Alec's music career would lead. We worried about Randall on his own in Europe. We feared Max was coming back from knee surgery too soon. And we miss Isaac, who now lives in Peoria. Those weren't choices I would have made, but history has proven that each decision was absolutely correct.

And I confess, I'm a little envious. I never got paid to play my guitar. Never slept in a Dublin hostel. Never won a championship medal. And never really moved away from home. But I totally love hearing their stories.

So it's really okay that they are not me. And it's okay that your son is not you.

Thankfully, my four sons have all followed my footsteps in one important area. They each have chosen a fabulous young woman with whom to share their life.

TAKEAWAY

If your son lives your life, what has he achieved?

"Orville Wright didn't have a pilot's license."
—Richard Tait

A Son Needs His Dad…

To Not Be Dazzled by the Digital Age

When I was in first or second grade, an older boy had me convinced that he had attached a rope to a rocket that he then shot into the moon, which he then pulled down into his backyard. (I was a trusting lad.) If memory serves, that fourth-grade windbag was the same con artist who pointed out the house where the witch lived and also talked me into touching my tongue to the frozen monkey bars. FYI: Your tongue really does stick to frozen metal pipes. And it really does hurt when you rip it away.

The tethered moon, the haunted house, losing a layer of skin off my tongue. My father never found out about any of those things. I should have told him. I could have. He would have explained the way the world works without making me feel stupid. Maybe I was embarrassed. Maybe I was trying to figure it out for myself. In any case, that's how it goes. For generations, even boys from good homes can and will be exposed to plenty of untruths. In most cases, no real harm done.

But today, untruths don't just come from the slick blowhard down the street. And today's lies will do more damage than causing a young boy to walk more quickly past an old lady's house or lick some icy playground equipment. Today's lies come faster and furious-er. They are packaged in slick images displayed on larger-than-life high-def screens or posted on much smaller screens transported in the pocket of most every teenage boy. And today's deceptions carry weightier consequences.

Despite what you may be thinking right now, this is not all bad news. Because as an informed, aware, and committed dad you understand the dangers. Your father didn't. Your father grew up in a safer, slower world. Your father's generation was amazed and intimidated by computer technology, digital graphics, and the accessibility of information. You, on the other hand, take it in stride and are well aware of how quickly a young man can get pulled into bad decisions that turn into bad habits that turn into lifelong or life-ending patterns.

So maybe the point is this. Dad, your father had an excuse for not rescuing you and your siblings from the accelerating culture of your youth. He was dazzled. The future was so bright, he wasn't prepared for it. But you've been warned. You experienced the first wave of intense, brain-piercing technology and have a justifiable fear concerning what's out there lurking and stalking your son. You know it's time to shield your eyes and help your son do the same.

So here's the plan. Get your son to be your teacher.

Unless you're in the business of developing or distributing digital media, you can't possibly stay better informed than your son when it comes to what's new and what's about to be new in the world of mass and social media. After all, your daily life is jam-packed with real-world adult responsibilities. Your son, however, has so much free time (and so many unused brain cells) that he consistently becomes an expert in technology that you don't even know exists.

So whether he's 9 or 19, go ahead and ask him about the latest technology. Of course, you may have to do a teensy bit of homework. You can't just say, "What's the latest gizmo?" He'll just say, "Nothing much." But if you can get a little specific and ask a real question that requires a real answer, there's a good chance he'll open up. Your assignment is to occasionally peruse tech websites. Research emerging technologies. Talk to other dads. Keep your eyes and ears open for buzz about the next messaging tool, gaming trend or networking innovation. Then ask your son about it. Treat him as an authority. Tell him you feel out of the loop and literally say, "Can you help me?" Then shut up and listen. Let him teach you.

The benefits are many. Time with your son. A chance to honor his accumulated knowledge. Letting him practice his own teaching skills. A smidgen of confidence for him. A dose of humility for you. Some new insight and abilities you might be able to actually use. And a portal into his world to see some of the good stuff and potentially bad stuff flowing into his life.

Maybe you'll learn something that might make your life easier or career path smoother. If so, give him credit. Maybe he'll introduce you to the latest gaming system that he's been enjoying over at a friend's house. If so, you've got some excellent insight for a birthday or Christmas present. Maybe you'll see something that has potential for delivering graphic violent or sexual content.

Let that new insight open the door to some father–son, teacher–student dialogue. Don't accuse him of shameful behavior, just bring it up. Because he has been side by side with you, you have the chance to ask an open-ended question: "Wow. So often technology has a dark side to it. Why does it have to be that way?" You may find his values align with yours more closely than you think. He just needs a little more time to nail them in place.

The best way to rescue your son from the dark side of technology is to come alongside him early and often. Establish your own high standards. Then be caring and courageous enough to point out dangerous choices or slippery slopes. Be a partner in his development. The goal is for him to establish, embrace, and defend his own high standards based on truth, experience, and everything he's learned from a dad he can trust.

TAKEAWAY

Over the course of their lives, our sons will make more decisions without us than with us. Which means we need to prepare them to be wise decision makers, not obedient order takers.

"Technology is so much fun but we can drown in our technology. The fog of information can drive out knowledge."
—Daniel J. Boorstin (1914–2004)

A Son Needs His Dad...

To Teach Him Stuff Your Dad Taught You

Things I learned growing up from my dad:

- Measure twice, cut once.
- Sand with the grain.
- How to tie a tie.
- How to jump-start a car.
- How to peel an apple.
- How to negotiate at a flea market.
- Release the emergency brake in a '66 Volkswagen before driving around town.
- How to play the old hidden ball trick.
- How to store a baseball glove over the winter.
- Catch a fly ball with two hands until after your rookie year in the majors.
- Shoot free throws using your left hand to guide and your right hand to push.
- Design a house and yard to minimize maintenance. No gutters to clean. No grass trimming. Cedar trim. Wood paneling that never needs painting.
- How to build a campfire.
- How to make s'mores.

- How to skip a stone.
- How to find the North Star, the Big Dipper, Orion's Belt, Sirius.
- There is order to the universe.
- Fold your hands to and from communion.
- Hide a key under the hood of your car for emergencies.
- Don't aim a gun at anything unless you intend to kill it.
- How to fill out a scorecard.
- Hundreds of baseball terms, including *squeeze play, sweet spot, bush league, Eephus pitch,* and *around the horn.*
- A disastrous Cubs season gives you something to look forward to next year.
- When planting a tree, dig a hole twice as big as the ball of roots— and water, water, water.
- How to organize a workshop.
- If two nails are sturdy, three nails are sturdier.
- The difference between a slotted and Phillips screwdriver.
- The difference between a monkey wrench, a Crescent wrench, and Vise-Grip pliers.
- Love your wife.
- Thank the cook.
- Respect the elderly.
- Have patience with kids who are trying hard, but just don't get it.
- An appreciation for old Clint Eastwood and Jimmy Stewart movies.
- How to put a worm on a hook.
- How to start an outboard engine.
- Be respectful and repentant when you get stopped by a police officer.

Making a list like this generates a boatload of memories. Mostly wonderful. Certainly a few regrets and missed opportunities. Including the stunning idea that I could have (should have) made this list three years ago and shared it with my dad before he died. Any father would like that. Including yours.

But really, the idea behind making this list was to remind dads they have skills, experience, and knowledge worth passing on. If those nuggets of wisdom started with you, that's fine. But if it's something that is being passed from father to son to son, go ahead and let your boy know that there's a generational connection to that lesson or strategy. Say, "This is something Grandpa Joe taught me when I was your age."

Finally, an apology to my four sons. Some of the items on the above list stopped with me. I learned them from Papa, but failed to pass all of them on to all of you. Hopefully I made up for that failure with a handful of other skills and tidbits I did successfully share with you.

Maybe someday you'll make a list and let me know.

TAKEAWAY

Most men look back on their lives without realizing how much they have given and how much they'll be missed.

"It doesn't matter who my father was, it matters who I remember my father was."

—Anne Sexton (1928–1974)

A Son Needs His Dad...

To Treat Him like a Future Dad

As a young boy in 1908, my grandfather Ferdinand immigrated with his family to America from Austria. At Ellis Island, his German-sounding last name was Americanized (slightly) to "Payleitner."

My dad had no brothers, and my brother has only daughters. Which means it's up to my four sons to keep alive Ferdinand's century-old lineage of the Payleitner name.

Mission accomplished.

That's right. While working on this manuscript, I became a dad of a dad. You can call me Gramps. I hope to get a few more, but Jackson David Payleitner is my first grandson. As you may imagine, that brings an entirely different perspective to a guy who's writing a book like this. When your son has a son, that's where the whole heritage-legacy adventure gets serious.

Now I did the best I could with Max. I can instantly recall quite a few blunders and things I would do differently. There were things I worried about that just didn't matter. And things I missed that I could have improved upon. But grace is a wonderful thing. Max married the perfect girl for him. And Megan delivered the perfect grandson for Rita and me. Of course, I might be a little biased.

It's fascinating to watch my son Max be a dad. He's still Max. Confident. Jubilant. Caring. Comfortable. A good friend. A protector and fierce competitor. But there's an entire new level of competence and awareness. He's really good with Jackson. Making him smile. Anticipating the needs of his wife and son. Jumping up when they need something. Walking around holding his infant son like a football is natural and easy. Clearly, Max is having no problem transitioning to fatherhood. Being a dad is something he always imagined he would be.

So what about the future dad living in your home? The best way to help your son imagine himself as a father is to pray for his wife and children. That's right. Not every night, but at bedtime go ahead and try praying something like,

"And heavenly Father, we'd also like to pray for Drew's life years from now. We don't know what the future holds, but you do. If that includes marriage and kids, that's fantastic. So we even pray right now for that little girl who will grow up to marry Drew. She's out there someplace. Would you protect her, Lord? Would you help her grow strong and wise, and introduce her to Drew at just the right time? Because you see all of eternity at once, Lord, we're even going to pray for their healthy kids who we trust will grow to love and serve you, Lord. Thank you so much that we can be confident in your plan..."

Is that weird? Not at all. If you pray like that with your seven-year-old son, he may think you're crazy. But he will fall asleep knowing you care and that God cares.

Of course, your son probably hasn't met his future bride. Alec, Randall, Max, and Isaac all met their wives after college. But maybe your son will end up marrying the little girl down the street. Or the bratty little sister of his best friend from middle school. In a twist of fate, your twentysomething son could fall in love with that really nice girl who was "just a friend" in high school. Whoever he picks out, love her like a daughter. Open your home and your family. Be extra nice to your son's in-laws. At holidays, don't force your grown children to come to your house. If you let them off the hook guilt-free, both your son and his bride will be always grateful. You're one big family now and grandchildren should bring you closer, not cause any jealousy or competition.

Speaking of that, Max and Megan did give my grandson the middle name of "David," which happens to be the first name of Megan's dad. I don't see that as a problem. Because, as stated above, his last name is Payleitner. Wow.

Jackson, you've already given me so much to be proud of.

Love, your buddy, Gramps.

TAKEAWAY

Next time your son does something that drives you crazy, envision him in just a few years as a dad. Maybe it will help you cut him some slack. Or if it feels right, you could even say, "Son, think about this for a second. Twenty years from now, do you want your son to be acting like this?" If he sees himself as a future husband and dad, it just might help his judgment today.

> *"Grandchildren are the crowning glory of the aged; parents are the pride of their children."*
>
> —PROVERBS 17:6 NLT

A Son Needs His Dad...

To Finish the Insect Collection

There's a term being kicked around in parenting magazines and social media that has decidedly negative connotations. I'm not sure it's as bad as the so-called experts make it out to be.

Here it is: "helicopter parenting."

Have you heard about it? Supposedly, helicopter parents swoop in and rescue their children from every difficult, uncomfortable, or undesirable circumstance.

Well, at a key moment for me in seventh grade, my dad was guilty of helicopter fathering. And I'm pretty sure it had a long and beneficial impact. Join me as we journey to Haines Junior High in the 1970s and together we'll decide if my well-intentioned dad did the right thing.

We had just moved to a new town and I suddenly found myself slightly overwhelmed by quite a few first-time experiences. Lockers with tricky combination locks. Gym class with mandatory group showers. A class schedule that had me moving to a different classroom every 50 minutes. Nine different teachers during the course of the week. And zero familiar faces.

Before the fall weather kicked in, one of the first assignments from biology teacher Mr. Tilton was an insect collection. The instructions—clearly printed in purple mimeograph ink—set forth a rubric requiring a minimum number of captured and chloroformed bugs, teeny-tiny hand-lettered informative cards, and three-inch straight pins strategically piercing the thorax of each and every dead bug.

I was clearly out of my league. It wasn't really impossibly difficult, except that I had sailed through six years of parochial school with very little effort. Suddenly Mr. Tilton was expecting me to take some initiative. I was being forced to read and follow instructions. Up until then, I could start most homework assignments the night before and grab an easy A-minus or B-plus.

We had two weeks to complete the assignment. In class, each student had assembled his or her very own "killing jar," which was pretty much a cotton ball doused with carbon tetrachloride in a pickle jar. The rest was homework. My strategy was a timeless one chosen by millions of students over the years. Especially boys. I stalled, delayed, and procrastinated.

On a warm fall Sunday afternoon, terror found me. The insect collection was due the next day. I had my trusty killing jar and a supply of entomologically approved pins, but that was about it. No box. No butterfly net. No plan. And no bugs.

My memory goes foggy here. I do remember confessing my crisis to my father. And I remember him instantly being able to interpret the lengthy and confusing instructions. I recall racing through the empty lot next door with pantyhose on a wire hanger and successfully swooping up a wide array of insects. I also remember arguing with my father that the cigar box he found wasn't big enough. And also insisting the bugs had to spend a specific amount of time in the killing jar. But I didn't put up too much of a fuss. By that time, I knew Dad's involvement was my only chance. I hand-lettered teeny-tiny cards while my dad and other family members identified bugs and told me what to write.

We finished well past my bedtime with a dozen properly pierced and labeled bugs. Mr. Tilton gave me an A.

That was more than 40 years ago and I still think about that insect collection more often than you might imagine. For the most part, I remember it as a positive experience. The family pitched in. Dad emphasizing how the finished product had to look just right. The deadline was met.

On the other hand, we threw the scientific process out the window. To this day, I rarely read recipes, directions, or any instruction box that pops up on my laptop screen. I never paid any penalty for procrastinating on my insect collection. Just ask my editor; he'll tell you that part of me is still a slacker. And I still carry a slight shred of guilt for not doing all the work myself.

So back to the original question. Is it wrong to rescue your son when his procrastination or bad choices puts himself in a position where failure is inevitable? What's the verdict on helicopter parenting?

How about this? If the looming failure may cause severe bodily or psychological injury, definitely swoop in *to the rescue*. If the failure is the result of a few minor missteps and unfortunate circumstances, *maybe* swoop in. If the failure will cause him to miss major opportunities for learning and growth in the immediate and distant future, swooping in for a rescue *may still be a good choice.*

But if a 12-year-old boy who has been skating by with little effort suddenly gets a failing grade on a project he really could have done by himself, then maybe that's a good thing. That reality check just might kick a promising young man to the next level of dedication and commitment to excellence. Put another way, if he leaves the assignment crinkled up in the bottom of his backpack, spends two weeks mastering a new video game, then lies to you about how hard he has been working, go ahead and let him fail.

I'm afraid, Dad, this is another one of those cases in which every kid and every situation is different. As for me, if my dad had allowed me to go to school that Monday without that completed (and masterfully rendered) insect collection, I might have learned a huge lesson and become a more hardworking student. But I would have missed something else. My appreciation for my dad jumped one notch higher that weekend. And what's that worth?

TAKEAWAY

Fatherhood is a constant stream of decisions large and small. Should I take that job in Denver and subject my family to another move? On the next vacation, should we drive straight through or stop at the historical sites and tourist traps? Should I read a bedtime story or watch the end of the Celtics game? I'm pretty sure that in 99 percent of the cases, the best answer is to make the choice that requires the most love.

> *"Make allowance for each other's faults, and forgive anyone who offends you. Remember, the Lord forgave you, so you must forgive others. Above all, clothe yourselves with love, which binds us all together in perfect harmony."*
>
> —Colossians 3:13-14 NLT

A Son Needs His Dad...

To Have Him Ditch School to Take Some Cuts in the Cage

School is important. Fathers need to emphasize that. Making school a priority is a lesson learned early. The first day of school is a big deal. Playing hooky is not an option. Even being in class when the bell rings shows proper respect for teachers and the educational process. Dads need to encourage their sons to take assignments seriously and show pride in their work. From papier-mâché volcanoes to doctoral dissertations. Every hour of the school day should be valued and maximized.

But taking Isaac out of school for six one-hour sessions in a batting cage with a professional hitting instructor was one of the best educational choices I ever made.

Here's how that unlikely scenario unfolded. With one exception, all four of my sons participated in high school football, wrestling, and baseball. Earning a total of 21 varsity letters. The last season of the last sport for my last son would be Isaac's varsity baseball season.

Isaac's wrestling career had been a success, but his final day on the mat was a heartbreaker. At regionals, he had to battle a bracket stacked against him, a few calls that didn't go his way, and a clock that ran out too soon. Suddenly his season was over two weeks earlier than we had hoped.

One of my most cherished photos was taken from across the gymnasium and captures former wrestlers Alec, Randy, and Max sitting beside their little brother on the bleachers just minutes after that final loss. After literally hundreds of matches, the Payleitner boys were done with wrestling.

In Illinois, the high-school sports seasons overlap a bit and so baseball was just around the corner. As a winter-sport athlete, Isaac was already behind many of his teammates who had been strengthening their throwing arms and perfecting their swing for months. Plus, the previous year Isaac had not cracked the starting lineup and was used primarily as a pinch runner. So his place on the team was up in the air.

After wrestling he was in great shape, but hitting a baseball takes more than just physical strength. So his dad made a suggestion. I knew he had already been accepted into the University of Illinois. And his class load for his final semester of high school was fairly light. So, I suggested he ditch a few hours of school—with his parents' permission—to sharpen his batting stance and swing for the fast-approaching season. We found the right instructor and scheduled a reasonable number of one-on-one lessons.

To make a long story short, during his senior season Isaac played every inning of every game in centerfield. He was among the team leaders in hits and RBIs and had more doubles than any other player in the county. In one doubleheader, he had a grand slam and ten RBIs. And he made the all-conference and all-area teams.

The lessons are many. Good wrestlers can make great ballplayers. Under the right circumstances, focused workouts with a professional trainer are worth the investment. Dads should look for opportunities to partner with their sons at their points of need. And of course, it was the disappointing end to one endeavor that helped springboard him into an award-winning experience later. Sometimes rain clouds do have a silver lining.

But the biggest lesson—one that's hard to convey to a child—is that Isaac earned the right to take off a few hours of classes. He had worked hard in the classroom for 12 and a half years and had proven himself to his parents and college admissions officers. Young people have a difficult time seeing how hard work today pays off in the future. That's where a dad who has built a relationship of trust with this son can come alongside him and say, "Finish your studies. Don't goof off in school. Put in a little extra effort now and it'll pay off in the long run."

TAKEAWAY

School is critically important. But the whole point of school is to set your son up for success later in life. Whether that's in a boardroom, in a laboratory, at a hospital, in a courtroom, or on a construction site. Or even on a baseball diamond in his senior year of high school.

"Education is not filling a bucket, but lighting a fire."
—William Butler Yeats (1865–1939)

A Son Needs His Dad...

To Pick Your Battles

O ur kids were not fussy eaters. But one of them really, really didn't like asparagus. Actually, none of the kids liked asparagus.

But during one particular dinner, one particular son let it be known that there was no way he was going to eat his asparagus. In my fatherly wisdom, I let it be known that he was not going to leave the dinner table without eating that asparagus. All four spears. It was a classic dinner-table standoff. I was serious and committed. So was he.

Truth be told, I like asparagus when it's steamed, buttered, and still hot. But—as you'll probably agree—cold and mushy asparagus is something on which to gag. And that's exactly what the young diner did. He sat there for several minutes, gave me the evil eye for several more, and finally shoved two or three cold, soggy asparagus spears into his mouth. Gagging, choking, and spitting some of the green goo back onto his plate.

That's all I remember. I don't recall how the incident ended. I believe that was the end of the standoff at the dining-room table and there was no additional punishment. I do remember suggesting to Rita that we quietly avoid serving asparagus for a while. We didn't tell that to the kids, but it just seemed like a battle we didn't want to fight again for a few months. And that was that.

That experience did not transform our entire parenting philosophy, but it did remind us that some battles are worth fighting. Some are not. Does your son hate asparagus, Brussels sprouts, liver, or beets? Of course he does. So why choose that battle? You certainly have that authority—if you think it's important—but then prepare to follow through to the end. When you do tell your son to do something with clarity and conviction, he has to know that you are absolutely committed to that ultimatum. If you choose a battle, then prepare yourself to fight that battle and win that battle.

Ultimatums, as you probably already know, are dangerous parenting tools. Rules change. New information becomes available. Kids mature. Every kid is different. Upon further review, some of your rules may not be that critical to success in life.

In the heat of a confrontation you might say, "If you get a tattoo, you are not welcome in this house." You might threaten, "Bring home a report card with a 'D' and your athletic career is over." Or you might say, "You're not leaving this table until that asparagus is gone." Do you really want your son to leave home forever, quit football, or fall asleep with his head in his dinner plate?

Still, you need to take a stand in some areas—absolutes that you and your son's mother need to agree on and enforce. For example: No drugs. No girls in his bedroom with the door shut. No cigarettes. No alcohol. No alcohol until he's 21. No video games with Teen or Mature ratings. No PG-13 movies. No R-rated movies. No NC-17 movies. No tattoos. No piercings. You can see how every family and every child is different. Again, make that call with your wife way ahead of time, and you'll have a fighting chance of enforcing that decree.

It's not easy, but you can even make something off-limits that they have already done.

"Your mother and I made a mistake. We let you go to that R-rated movie, but we shouldn't have. Until you're 16, don't ask to go to another R-rated film unless it's something that has value to it."

"Last night, Carly was up in your bedroom with the door closed. We didn't want to embarrass you last night. But that can't happen again."

"Yes, I smoked pot. I messed up. I threw away some opportunities because of it. Son, one of my responsibilities is to keep you from making the same mistake."

So pick your battles wisely. Try to choose issues that matter and battles you can win. Enlisting the aid of other parents helps a great deal. If every kid in town is doing something, it's hard for your son to be out of the loop. But that doesn't make it right. And it's really okay to let your son know that you have high expectations.

You love him. And you would do anything to protect him. He knows that, right?

—— TAKEAWAY ——

Remember, the goal is not for you to win the battle and for your son to lose the battle. The goal is for your son to join your side.

"As a child my family's menu consisted of two choices: take it, or leave it."
—BUDDY HACKETT (1924–2003)

A Son Needs His Dad…

To Always, Always, Always Have an Inflating Needle Handy

Your son and a small huddle of his buddies—somewhere between the age of 4 and 34—come to your backyard, street, or driveway to participate in a sport that requires a ball that requires air.

That's a good thing.

It doesn't matter if they're future hall-of-famers or absolutely laughable. When guys get together to play rugby, football, basketball and, yes, even soccer, it's a great event. Worth celebrating.

Then tragedy strikes. Your son's pals and the ball are deflated—literally and figuratively. They have the lifeless ball. They have a working air pump. But they desperately need one of those precious two-inch silver inflating needles. How will the crisis be resolved?

Your son confidently knows the answer is right inside the house. It's you, Dad. You're about to be hero of the realm. He interrupts your nap or your newspaper and explains the need.

Dad, all you have to do is reach into the tin can on your workbench, the cuff-link dish in your walk-in closet, or your top desk drawer and pull out that shiny little implement and silently hand it over.

"Thanks, Dad! You're the best." Even if he doesn't say it, he'll think it.

You do have one, don't you? You'd better. If not, I suggest you head out on your lunch break today and pick one up. Or two. Or three. Stash them where you can find them, but they can't. In their time of need, you want them to come to you.

Meeting the needs of their children in the immediate and long-term. That's what dads do.

That means protecting them. Providing for them. Helping them dream big dreams. Teaching them right from wrong. Having the right tool at the right time. Including a 99-cent inflating needle.

Two last thoughts. Remind your son or daughter to spit on the inflating needle before inserting. And don't miss the chance to get out there yourself and offer to play all-time quarterback.

═══════════════ **TAKEAWAY** ═══════════════

Do this. Seriously. Write yourself a note. Send yourself a text. Today or tomorrow, secure possession of an inflating needle. You'll be so glad you did.

> *"Some people want it to happen, some wish it would happen, others make it happen."*
>
> —MICHAEL JORDAN (1963–)

A Son Needs His Dad…

To Teach Him the True Purpose of Competition

For ten years, I coached beginning wrestling. Boys in kindergarten through second grade in gym shorts and T-shirts would gather in a real wrestling room to learn real wrestling. Parents lined the perimeter of the room, including quite a few hesitant moms who seemed unsure about the whole thing. Our first session together was always my favorite.

I'd set the tone with a sharp blow of my coach's whistle and bark my first order to "Circle up!" Then, surrounded by eager young faces, I treated them with respect and let them know I had high expectations. That morning I had five goals.

First, let them know it was an honor to be wrestler. It took discipline and mental toughness. If they stuck with it, I promised them success as individuals and as a team.

Second, clarify a misconception. I would ask for a show of hands: "How many of you have seen WWF pro wrestling with guys in costumes and long hair screaming at each other in a boxing ring?" Almost every hand would go up. I would silently turn a complete circle, making eye contact with each young wrestler, and with quiet conviction say, "Gentlemen, this…is not that. That is fake. They are actors. The wrestling you are about to experience is real."

Third, teach them the most important part of every match: the handshake. To hundreds of boys, I demonstrated a firm grip, eye contact, and a single pump. Then I made them practice with each other. Only in wrestling do competitors shake hands before and after every match.

Fourth, since many of them had never witnessed a real match, I would invite two older, experienced wrestlers to demonstrate how the sport is about control, not showmanship. In the simplest terms, they would learn about the two ways to win a wrestling match: by scoring more points than your opponent after three periods or by pin. One of the amazing things about wrestling is that even if you're losing the match with just seconds remaining, you still have a chance to win by pinning the wrestler's shoulders to the mat for just two seconds. Which means it's important to keep wrestling until the last whistle.

Finally, after demonstrating my sincerity and gaining their trust I would quietly pose my favorite question for novice wrestlers: "What do you think? Is winning important? Is it important to win?" The boys would look around, slightly unsure of how to respond. Invariably, a few of them would say, "No."

I loved that moment. Clearly those boys had been watching too much Barney the purple dinosaur or been exposed to too much wimpy talk about playing fair and not being too aggressive from some saccharine preschool teacher. As their first wrestling coach, I took it upon myself to correct their inaccurate perception.

My little speech would go something like this: "Gentlemen, let me tell you about winning. Winning is important. Winning is a good thing. Winning a wrestling match or any competition in any sport is the goal. That's why we practice, listen, learn, work, and sweat. Your goal is to improve. To learn. To get strong so that you can win your next match. It's fun to win. I like to win. Do you like to win? Does your mom or dad want you to win? When you go out there and shake the hand of your opponent is it your goal to lose or to win?"

Now by this time, the boys are eager and excited. The troops have been rallied. They're responding with yeses and cheers. Then with a rising tone that would make Knute Rockne proud, I ask the initial question one more time, "So! Is winning important?" With fervor, some of them even jump to their feet and shout, "YES!"

That's when I'd stop. And in a much calmer voice I would say, "I agree. Winning is important. But I'm wondering if there are some things that are even more important than winning?" That's when the light would go on. Those sharper-than-you-might-think elementary-school boys would propose mature concepts like "doing your best…working hard…being a good sport…family…friends…teamwork…shaking hands." And, I would respond, "Yes, yes, yes, and yes! Winning is important, but there are things that are even more important."

Over the years, some of those young wrestlers responded with surprising answers. A few boys said, "God is more important than wrestling." With delight, I added my affirmation. One boy said, "Music." After a pause, I said, "Yes. Music and art and other beautiful things are probably more important than winning a wrestling match." One eloquent young man said, "Trying hard and then losing and trying hard again is more important than winning." That's good stuff.

Remember now, parents always stuck around for the first session. Never did any mom or dad try to stop me in the middle of my lesson on winning. Thank goodness. But many of them would come up after this session or at the end of the season to express their thanks. Being a coach who has the right priorities is an unforgettably rewarding experience.

Some of those young wrestlers went on to earn medals, trophies, and college scholarships. Others simply burned off some boyhood energy during a winter's worth of Saturday mornings. All of them, I hope, got a dose of what it means to set priorities and meet a challenge head-on. That's a principle that applies in any endeavor they ever choose to tackle.

TAKEAWAY

It took me several years to perfect this approach that blends teaching sportsmanship with a winning attitude. If you try it with a group of boys, let me know how it works. The principle also works one-on-one with your own son.

"Once you've wrestled, everything else in life is easy."
—DAN GABLE (1948–)

A SON NEEDS HIS DAD...

To Purchase the Entire Wendy's Dollar Menu. Twice.

This is not a recommendation. It is merely an example. With that caveat, allow me to tell a story.

My sons Randy and Max are three-and-a-half years apart. Of my five kids, they were definitely the most antagonistic toward each other from toddler age through middle school. When Randy headed off to college, suddenly Max missed his sparring partner. As their time together became more precious, their sibling rivalry somehow morphed into a deep and abiding friendship. As a dad, it blessed me to see it.

Still, the competitiveness remained. One perfect summer evening the boys were extolling the virtue, value, and tastiness of the Wendy's dollar menu.

Somehow speculation began regarding whether or not it was possible for one individual to consume one of everything on that menu, including three burgers, one chicken sandwich, chicken nuggets, chili, fries, baked potato, salad, Frosty, and beverage of choice—all in one sitting.

Somehow that idea morphed into a contest pitting the 17-year-old against the 20-year-old in a contest of wills and stomach-stretching. Somehow Dad paid for the entire event.

The folks at Wendy's should be glad we didn't use their dining room. Instead the sacks of fast food were spread out on our picnic table while friends and family gathered for the unlikely competitive feast. Details are sketchy. I do remember it wasn't pretty. Years later, both boys claim some kind of victory. But the truth is Randy and Max both wisely gave up with a few burgers still left in their wrappings.

It was probably the best $22 plus tax I spent that summer. The howls of laughter still echo through our backyard and family room.

Bragging rights remain unclaimed. But I'll claim victory for dads everywhere.

The sheer joy of allowing such a foolhardy event to take place is a reward that some dads may never experience. Maybe those fathers are too uptight. Maybe they don't foster enough silliness in their children. Maybe their kids are wonderfully silly, but don't feel comfortable expressing silliness in front of their parents.

If I'm describing you, loosen up, Dad. When a bizarre idea pops up with family or friends, consider the worst-case scenario. If there's no threat to life or limb, shake your head, say, "You guys are crazy," but then quickly add, "Let's do it."

TAKEAWAY

Common sense and silliness cannot co-exist. Sometimes choose one, sometimes choose the other.

"What is comedy? Comedy is the art of making people laugh without making them puke."

—STEVE MARTIN (1945–)

A Son Needs His Dad…

To Think Before You Click

D o you sometimes want to scream at television and the Internet because all they seem to deliver is sex, greed, vulgarity, and stupidity? Well, guess what? The reason all that stuff is so pervasive is because it's so popular.

Look at a list of the top 20 television shows and—without mentioning any titles—it seems like most of them feature creepy people doing creepy things. I like TV. I like the idea of pushing a couple of buttons on a remote control and having creative, amusing, and thought-provoking stories and people enter my living room for an evening of entertainment. But I don't want to feel like I have to take a shower afterward.

If I'm sitting alone at my desk and researching anything—financial advice, used cars, parenting wisdom, movie reviews, lacrosse, lasagna, vacations, how to throw a curveball, when to change your transmission fluid, or who was president during the Great Depression—I don't want to be fearful of where I look and where I click. But careful we must be. Something ugly, perverse, or repugnant is always three mouse clicks away. And it's amazing how often we men will click, click, click, and allow that kind of crud to pop up on our screens. (If you are strong enough to avoid the crud, at least admit that much of the stuff that you see online is an unfortunate waste of time.)

Anyway. One of the time-tested principles of media is that whatever attracts response leads to more of the same. In the 1950s, the first-edition comic books that sold were the ones that became long-running series. In the 1980s, movie producers discovered the high profitability of sequels and responded by giving us such nonclassics as *Gremlins 2, Grease 2, Ghostbusters II*, and *Lethal Weapon 2*. In the 2000s, the success of *Survivor, Big Brother*, and *American Idol* quickly led to a plethora of painful copycat reality TV shows that created celebrities who had zero talent and zero self-respect.

Continuing my rant. Whatever sells, sells. What we click on, we get more of. That's not surprising.

Now here's where it gets scary, especially for fathers who are trying to raise sons with some sense of moral grounding and a hope for a slightly brighter future.

It used to be that nationwide ratings and overall box-office sales were the determining factor for what images came to your living room or local theater. Similarly, mass quantities of "likes" and "views" determined what was watched on YouTube and other social media outlets.

Dad, we're now at a crossroads. Tracking software and preference analysis doesn't just send you what the world seems to want, it guesses what you want and sends you more of it. For the most part, your clicks and viewing choices today determine what you will be offered tomorrow. If there's more and more crud coming your way, there's a good chance you invited it. That's just a little frightening, isn't it?

You know that as a father, you need to protect your children and help provide a pathway through childhood into productive, life-affirming adulthood. Sons especially follow in their father's footsteps. That used to mean going into the family business and nurturing the next generation.

You may or may not pass your plumbing business or passion for teaching on to your son, but your legacy still runs deep, influencing the very core of your son's values and morals. Integrity begets integrity. Abuse begets abuse. Bigotry begets bigotry. Knowledge-seekers beget knowledge-seekers. A creative spark begets a creative spark.

The course of action is clear. Don't fear media. Don't move off the grid to a shack in the middle of nowhere. Instead, make choices you and your family can live with. Be aware and steer clear of images and ideas that drag you down. The slope is getting steeper and slipperier. And the next generation is going to get more of what you choose.

The Bible challenges us, "Whatever is true, whatever is noble, whatever is right, whatever is pure, whatever is lovely, whatever is admirable—if anything is excellent or praiseworthy—think about such things" (Philippians 4:8). As always, when you look to the Scriptures for answers, you'll find them.

Maybe this is all good news. Because of the way technology tracks our individual lives, we may no longer be able to influence what content is delivered to our neighbors or the rest of the world. But we can now actually help determine what comes into our own home.

━━━━━━━━━━━━━━━━━━ TAKEAWAY ━━━━━━━━━━━━━━━━━━

It's always been true that our lives and choices influence the next generation. But that impact often did not show up for decades. Today's technology speeds up every aspect of our lives, serving as an instant mirror that reflects our choices back to us and into the hearts and minds of our children.

"If we continue to develop our technology without wisdom or prudence, our servant may prove to be our executioner."
—OMAR BRADLEY (1893–1981)

A Son Needs His Dad…

To Buy a Unicycle

There's a unicycle hanging from the ceiling in our garage. I know that because I bump my head on it two or three times every summer. It's barely been ridden. And that's okay.[1]

We bought it for Randy's ninth birthday for about 75 bucks. He gave it a try, spending maybe six or eight hours goofing with it, all told. His brothers and sister also spent varying amounts of time experimenting with the one-wheeled contraption. Isaac probably stayed up the longest—eight or ten seconds. None of them ever really got the hang of it, and the unicycle now hangs in my garage as a memorial to one of the great secrets of being a dad.

I am absolutely sure that out of my five children, one or two had the physical agility and mental acuity to become an expert unicyclist. Again, it's not easy. It would have taken hours of practice, perhaps an entire summer. I certainly am not going to blame any of my kids for not following through. The mental gyroscope required for mastering the unicycle cannot be detected by visual inspection. Plus, I don't think any of them ever caught the vision of how cool it would be to ride down the street on one wheel.

So whether they knew it or not, each of them did a cost-benefit analysis of the time it would take, the amount of frustration they might endure, Dad's expectations, the reality that it might not even be possible, and the immediate and long-term usefulness of having that particular skill. Any of them had a legitimate chance to go for it and master it. But each of them chose not to.

In those pivotal magic summers, during which maturing pre-teens have few responsibilities and many options, they each decided their time was better spent elsewhere. Their choices were the same choices made by generations of young people: playing rundown, swimming, riding two-wheeled bikes, tree-climbing, inventing backyard games, watching the Cubs lose on WGN, tormenting their siblings, hanging out with friends, and maybe even reading a book or two. All reasonable, typical, healthy choices.

Does that mean I failed as a father? Of course not. Actually, that unicycle proves that I was fulfilling one of the great responsibilities of being a dad. A privilege we have that no one else can do better.

Dads open doors. We place new opportunities in front of our sons, do a little song-and-dance sell job, and then get out of the way. We can instruct them, but we can't do it for them. We can sign them up and even insist they give it a try, but we can't flip that little switch in their brain that says, "I have found my life's passion." We can spark a vision, but we shouldn't try to live vicariously through them.

You know what I'm talking about. You wrestled in high school, so you install a regulation wrestling mat in your basement hoping your son becomes a state champ. You buy a baby grand piano confident your son is going to be the next Franz Liszt or Michael W. Smith. You see some talent in your son for visual arts, so you run out and buy paint and an art easel, envisioning a gallery of masterpieces signed by your son.

Even if none of those things come even close to happening, don't you dare call it a fail. As a matter of fact, it may be just the opposite. The wrestling mat, piano, and art easel may actually be a conduit for some unexpected activity that does bring a new vision to your son's life. Somersaulting on that mat—not wrestling—may lead to a career as a world-class gymnast. The kid who lives down the street may drop by and noodle on that piano, motivating your son to write lyrics to songs that end up on Broadway. The primary use for the art easel may turn out to be holding a giant sketchpad for Pictionary. As emcee for those party games, your son finds his niche as a motivational speaker or game-show host.

Only God knows how all of life's pieces fit together. As fathers, we're called to keep opening doors of opportunity and experience for our children. Some will slam closed—many will remain open for years and then gently swing shut. Still others will open wide to real-life laboratories, classrooms, boardrooms, gymnasiums, galleries, and auditoriums.

So no regrets. Without hesitation, my recommendation to any dad of a nine-year-old is "buy him a unicycle." The very worst that happens is he is forced to make a choice. Not a failure. Just a choice.

And who knows? Your son might just master the one-wheeled beast, run away, and join the circus.

=== TAKEAWAY ===

All we can do is open doors for our sons. They are going to choose to walk through them or not. And that's okay.

> *"Fortune knocks at every man's door once in a life, but in a good many cases the man is in a neighboring saloon and does not hear her."*
>
> —MARK TWAIN (1835–1910)

A SON NEEDS HIS DAD...

To Get a New Hobby

All of our kids competed in several sports, which meant Rita and I clocked a lot of hours standing on sidelines and sitting in bleachers. I couldn't begin to count how many miles we put on minivans driving to soccer fields, baseball diamonds, and gymnasiums over 25 years. But for season after season, that was how we spent virtually every Saturday morning and Sunday afternoon. Often it was the entire family going to support one athlete. Other times it was divide and conquer. Mom went to one field; dad went to a gym across town. The siblings came along as built-in automatic cheering sections.

There's a good chance you know the drill. In the car, you kick around offensive and defensive strategies. Before games, you watch how your kids interact with their teammates. During games, you see how they challenge themselves to the next level of competitiveness. After a victory, you leave the parking lot boisterously celebrating a few key plays. After a loss, the young athlete might not want to talk about the game for a few miles. As parents, we wait for just the right time to break the silence and still celebrate a few key plays. Then we begin to anticipate the next opportunity.

And it wasn't just sports. For the Payleitners, you can add band concerts, mock-trial events, chess tournaments, science fairs, and speech contests. I'm not bragging, I'm remembering. Even though those hundreds of trips have now become a blur, my memory tells me we won more than we lost, but I could be mistaken. I choose to remember the positives.

That's what a dad does, right? We celebrate, console, and look to the future with optimism.

When the kids were younger I would often ask God to guide me as a father. "Lord, help me be the kind of dad you want me to be." Whether it was an extended prayer during a sleepless night or a quick prayer while packing the car, God's reply was always the same. He would give me a kind of core fathering formula: "For the next season of life, put your kids before yourself." I heard, but I was never sure what that meant.

You see, I had been a selfish kind of guy. And I was sure that God had great things planned for me. Why suddenly would he want me to put my own interests on the back burner? Then it hit me. My kids had become my hobby. Was that a good thing? Was that healthy?

In my early 20s, I had designed and built some furniture—a coffee table, bookcase, a few coat trees. I had played some golf, rugby, and softball. I had done a little writing. A little acting. A little guitar. But as soon as the kids started getting involved in their own extracurricular activities, my hobbies instantly lost their appeal.

There's not one smidge of regret. It became a joy and privilege to be anywhere and everywhere my children were involved—volunteering, coaching, practicing, carpooling, serving on boards, or just sitting in the audience or bleachers.

Sometimes I even seemed out of place, but my kids were mostly fine with it. I recall a middle-school field trip to the Chicago Historical Society with eight parents as chaperones—seven moms and me. At one out-of-town freshman B-level baseball game in the sleet, I was the only fan in attendance. Like many elementary-school students, our kids were often involved in presentations and performed skits intended for an audience of classmates only. More than once Rita and I snuck into the back of the classroom to watch. Teachers didn't mind at all.

Over the years, I have heard other parents put down mothers and fathers who "drop everything for their kids" or "don't have their own life." My unspoken response was always that I felt sorry for those parents. They were missing out. The lasting images and lasting connections made with Alec, Randy, Max, Isaac, and Rae Anne are worth every trip across town and every lost weekend.

Like so many fathering ideas in this book, there's a flip side. And it's this. Your current hobby may actually be the best resource you have to connect with your kids. Maybe your pastime or passion can be something you do together. If you can walk 18 holes with your middle-school son and not want to kill him, go for it. If you get jazzed about stock cars or the stock market, invite your son into that world. If he picks up on it, what great conversations you'll have about pistons or portfolios over the next 60 years. If he shows authentic interest in your hobby of stamp collecting, motorcycle restoration, ham radio, building ships in bottles, geocaching, or paintball, then invite him along.

So one way or another, make your son your hobby. If that sounds weird, try this instead: For now, put his needs before yours. He'll be up, out, and gone before you know it. While he's under your roof, you'll be glad you invested the best part of your life into his.

━━━━━━━━━━━━━━━━━ **TAKEAWAY** ━━━━━━━━━━━━━━━━━

Time spent with your son is never wasted. Very likely, it becomes the very experience that inspires and propels the next season of your own life.

> *"Time is free, but it's priceless. You can't own it, but you can use it. You can't keep it, but you can spend it. Once you've lost it you can never get it back."*
> —HARVEY MACKAY (1932–)

A Son Needs His Dad...

To Be the Smartest Man in the World

My new grandson, Jackson, is a fifth-generation Chicago Cubs fan. No jokes are necessary. We've heard them all. Also, please don't feel sorry for us. When you count up those five generations of Payleitner men, it's an honor and a privilege to represent the middle link. I can look back and picture my father and grandfather sitting at Wrigley. And I can look into the future and see me, Max, and Jack.

We never had season tickets. But during those critical years when a boy develops team loyalty, my dad made sure we made at least two or three pilgrimages every summer to the shrine at the corner of Clark and Addison Streets.

One of the great traditions for my brother and me was filling out our own scorecards with two fresh, sharp Cubs pencils purchased from one of the vendors just inside the Wrigley Field turnstiles. In the 1960s, the scorecards were a quarter and the pencils were a dime. We never asked our dad for foam fingers, Cubs pennants, or Billy Williams jerseys. We knew that the scorecard and pencil were our souvenirs. And that was enough.

About the second inning of one of those games, tragedy struck. My pencil lead broke. Of course I could sharpen it at home, but how was I going to complete my traditional duties tracking Kessinger, Beckert, Williams, Banks, Santo, Hundley, and company? I couldn't ask for another pencil, could I?

I showed the unusable writing utensil to my dad and he didn't miss a beat. He took it and within 20 seconds handed it back sharpened and ready for the next batter. You may be able to guess what he did. To an adult, it may seem obvious. But to this nine-year-old, scraping that pencil at just the right angle with just the right pressure against the concrete floor of the grandstand was nothing short of brilliant. My dad was a genius!

Dad, for a season of life, you too are a genius. It won't always be that way. There will come a time—hopefully—when your son knows more than you. But for a while, you want to be the one man he looks up to who can solve any crisis large or small.

When your son panics because he needs to paint a green dragon but only has paint in primary colors, you show him how to mix blue and yellow. He'll be astonished.

When the printer cartridge is running low as he prints out a 12-page homework assignment, you know that a gentle shake will loosen up the toner to finish the job. He'll be relieved.

When the Little League baseball game comes to a screeching halt because the loudmouth coach from the other dugout and the 12-year-old umpire can't agree on the rules, you're the quiet voice of reason that walks out to the infield and calmly explains the infield fly rule. He'll be proud.

The key to being a genius, of course, is to be nonchalant. To act like no problem is too big. No challenge too great. You are the man with the answers.

While you can, I urge you to store up genius points. There will come a time when the challenges of life get a bit more complicated and solutions are a little more difficult. There will also come a time when you'll be asking your son for help with a minor emergency or puzzling challenge. And that's not a bad thing. Actually, there's a satisfying sense of fulfillment when life comes full circle and your son comes to the rescue of his old man.

But for now, be the smartest man in the world. That's a great gift for a young boy. To know that his dad can beat any other dad. At least when it comes to cleverness, wisdom, logic, and wits.

TAKEAWAY

Life lessons don't always have to be spoken. A better choice may be to sharpen that broken pencil, straighten that bent nail, or start the campfire without a single word. A genius lets his actions speak for themselves.

"Any fool can make something complicated.
It takes a genius to make it simple."
—WOODY GUTHRIE (1912–1967)

A Son Needs His Dad...

To Bequeath Some Mad Skills

I taught my four sons and one daughter to juggle the summer after each of them finished sixth grade. Before that age, they likely didn't have the cognitive and physical capacity to perform the required tossing, catching, reacting, focusing, and so on. After that age, they may have been distracted by other pursuits of youth.

The actual act of juggling three tennis balls is not really that difficult. You need a good instructor (like me), a mere one hour of instruction, some time by yourself to practice, and maybe 15 minutes of follow-up instruction that includes reminders, tips, and minor adjustments in technique. After that, it's really up to you, the juggler, to improve on the craft.

For boys with a smidge of hand-eye coordination it's an impressive skill that's fairly easy to master. Juggling butcher knives, flaming torches, or more than three objects is quite a bit more difficult and quite unnecessary. Tossing, catching, and circulating three baseballs in the air while he waits his turn in the batting cage captures your son an easy audience. Once he gains some confidence, let him know that the key is to be nonchalant about it. Never say, "Look what I can do." Just do it. As you can imagine, it's an especially helpful skill for boys who are a little shy or not so good with words. He will soon discover that 20 seconds of confident juggling will draw a smattering of applause or mild appreciation. Not a bad thing.

If he shows any appreciation for this gift you have given him, go ahead and remind your son of two key life truths. One, less is more. Two, confidence is a worthy attribute, but don't let it expand your reach into dangerous territory. In other words, juggling kiwis at a fruit stand or cell phones at an AT&T kiosk is not recommended.

Helping your son acquire a slightly difficult skill that his friends don't have has a high return on your investment of time and creativity. Examples beyond juggling? Reciting the alphabet backward. Reciting all the presidents in eight seconds. Whistling with your fingers. Nunchucks. Mastering a few simple magic tricks. Or card tricks. Rubik's cubing. Playing the spoons. Or just being confident in reciting a short poem or quotation. I recommend "Stopping by Woods on a Snowy Evening" by Robert Frost, Teddy Roosevelt's speech that begins "It's not the critic who counts," or the ever-valuable twenty-third psalm.

In some ways, such learned skills are not prestigious or groundbreaking. But doesn't happiness often come in small moments? Moments that break the monotony of a lumbering day. Moments that relieve the tension of a high-stress situation. Moments when we are recognized as individuals. Moments that don't change the course of history, but may launch new relationships and forge new friendships.

Of course, your son's life achievements should extend beyond playground feats, parlor tricks, and brainteasers. Once he gets noticed, he'll want to bring to the table some skills and expertise that have real-life value. Let's face it, the ballplayer who keeps the team loose by juggling during warm-up drills and then gets the game-winning hit is worthy of double honor.

So continue to encourage him to study, practice, sweat, think deep thoughts, keep his nose to the grindstone, and burn the midnight oil to become the best at what he wants to do with his life. But there's no guilt or shame in mastering two or three silly attention-getters so that—at the right time and place—he gets some attention and livens up the day for some friend, stranger, teammate, or family member who needs some perking up.

TAKEAWAY

If your son is already the class clown, then ignore this short chapter. But if he's a little shy or the only side he has is serious, then put some intentional effort into bequeathing him a totally useless skill.

"It is not the critic who counts, not the man who points out how the strong man stumbled, or where the doer of deeds could have done better. The credit belongs to the man who is actually in the arena; whose face is marred by the dust and sweat and blood; who strives valiantly; who errs and comes

*short again and again; who knows the great enthusiasms, the
great devotions and spends himself in a worthy cause; who at
the best, in the end, knows the triumph of high achievement,
and who, at worst, if he fails, at least fails while daring
greatly; knowing that his place shall never be among those
cold and timid souls who know neither victory nor defeat."*

—THEODORE ROOSEVELT (1858–1919)

A Son Needs His Dad…

To Be His Sparring Partner

In a very real way, sons need to do battle with their fathers.[2] As he prepares to make his mark in the world, a boy needs to take stock of his own abilities, measuring himself against the man who forever will be the prototype for what it means to be a husband, father, protector, and provider. That's you, Dad.

Doing battle with your son is not about breaking his spirit, butting heads maliciously, wielding your authority unfairly, or trampling his manhood. If that's where you're headed, exit that road quickly. Your job is to be a good sparring partner—figuratively and perhaps even literally.

Preparing for an upcoming bout, a boxer will spend hours in the practice ring with his sparring partner. Their goal is not to do physical harm to each other—instead it's to hone their skills, get into the best shape possible, and discover their own best strategies for victory. Does your son need to work on his jab, uppercut, or roundhouse? How are his footwork and blocking? Can he deliver a knockout punch? We can beat the metaphor to death, but suffice it to say, practice makes perfect. Because you care so much about your son, you are the ideal foil to help him determine his strengths and weaknesses while competing in a safe environment.

In the ring, sparring partners sometimes go half or three-quarter speed to allow their colleague to work on strategic moves. Both boxers are well protected with headgear and extra padding. Both boxers grow in the process without risk. Just so, a father can challenge his son in any physical or intellectual competition and both of you will gain wisdom and experience in the battle.

In early competitions, Dad should expect to emerge victorious. As the years pass, the goal is for the son to prevail more and more often.

Should a father ever reduce his effort to let his son win? My recommendation is no. Your son will know right away if you're not doing your best.

Then when they do eventually earn an authentic victory over their old man, they'll never know for sure, and the significance will be lost. On the other hand, can a father manipulate circumstances so that a young warrior gets a taste of victory at an early age? Absolutely. Be clever. Be wise. Be humble and gracious in defeat.

Examples? In one-on-one father–son basketball, let's say your middle-schooler is playing the game of his young life and the score is very close. On your next few jump shots, see if you can muster all your skills to bounce your shot off the back of the rim and into his waiting hands for the rebound. Afterward, shake his hand and let him enjoy his victory, perhaps tolerating just a tiny bit of playful trash talk. Just make sure you dominate in the next few games. You don't want him to get too cocky.

In chess, if your son has been improving his skills by playing with peers, then maybe he has earned the right to taste victory against Dad. Don't ignore your favorite strategies and certainly don't "accidentally" leave key pieces unprotected. Instead, simply don't use all the weapons in your arsenal, such as those strategies you learned from that old Russian chess master who hid in your attic during the Cold War. In other words, go three-quarter speed and see if your son rises to the challenge. It takes real artistry to throw a game of chess (or checkers) without your opponent realizing it.

Pick a competition, any competition. Soon enough he'll be beating your pants off. Then, because of your role as sparring partner, you can even take a small amount of credit for his improvement. Also, it will be ever so much sweeter each time he claims victory against one of his peers.

For now, go ahead and dominate in Ping-Pong and Scrabble. It's to your son's advantage if his father catches more fish, hits a straighter drive, or stacks a higher house of cards. As long as you can outperform him, do it. It will give the young man something to shoot for and a reason to keep asking you to play. Just don't forget to celebrate when he passes you by.

By the way, none of this applies to video games. Not once will you beat him. Unless he lets you.

=============== **TAKEAWAY** ===============

Be the kind of competitor you want your son to be. Tenacious. Spirited. Honest. Humble. Courageous. Willing to practice. Eager to learn.

Show appreciation when he hits a great backhand volley. Cheer when he sinks that birdie putt. You may have just found a worthy adversary to play once a week for the next 40 years.

> *"I cheat my boys every chance I get. I trade with the boys and skin 'em and I just beat 'em every time I can. I want to make 'em sharp."*
>
> —JOHN D. ROCKEFELLER (1839–1937)

A Son Needs His Dad...

To Finally Grasp That Poem You Read Back in High School

There's a good chance you read the poem "If—" by Rudyard Kipling back in some freshman English class and never really gave it much thought. At best, you remember something about a moral lesson that seemed a little preachy. If your teacher made you research author background, you may recall that Kipling grew up in and around Bombay back when India was part of the British Empire. But mostly, his name rings a bell because he wrote *The Jungle Book,* the collection of original stories that was Disney-fied in 1967. Before you start whistling "The Bare Necessities," I invite you to take another look at the poem. Keep an open mind and take your time. Now that you're a man and a dad, I promise it will knock your socks off. As you read, pretend you're speaking to your son.

> If you can keep your head when all about you
> Are losing theirs and blaming it on you,
> If you can trust yourself when all men doubt you,
> But make allowance for their doubting too:
> If you can wait and not be tired by waiting,
> Or being lied about, don't deal in lies,
> Or being hated, don't give way to hating,
> And yet don't look too good, nor talk too wise:
>
> If you can dream—and not make dreams your master;
> If you can think—and not make thoughts your aim;
> If you can meet with Triumph and Disaster
> And treat those two impostors just the same;

If you can bear to hear the truth you've spoken
Twisted by knaves to make a trap for fools,
Or watch the things you gave your life to, broken,
And stoop and build 'em up with worn-out tools;

If you can make one heap of all your winnings
And risk it on one turn of pitch-and-toss,
And lose, and start again at your beginnings,
And never breathe a word about your loss;
If you can force your heart and nerve and sinew
To serve your turn long after they are gone,
And so hold on when there is nothing in you
Except the Will which says to them: "Hold on!"

If you can talk with crowds and keep your virtue,
Or walk with Kings——nor lose the common touch,
If neither foes nor loving friends can hurt you,
If all men count with you, but none too much;
If you can fill the unforgiving minute
With sixty seconds' worth of distance run,
Yours is the Earth and everything that's in it,
And—which is more—you'll be a Man, my son!

I am no English teacher, but I hope you'll allow me to paraphrase.

Know who you are. Understand that really the only thing you can control is your own heart, mind, and actions. Don't be swayed from your honor by others.

Dream big, but think before you act. And don't get too full of yourself. Life brings good and bad. How you respond makes all the difference.

When the dust settles on your life, take responsibility. Be humble in victory. Be restrained in loss. When faced with an impossible task, resolve to respond beyond your ability.

It's relationships that matter. And our time on Earth is short. Your life has infinite value, but of even greater value is your integrity.

Now don't you wish you had paid better attention back in high school? A thorough understanding of Kipling's poem might have saved you from all those not-so-good decisions you made in your early twenties.

The good news is that you now have a new weapon in your arsenal to use during those late-night man-to-man talks with your son. If you don't have such talks now, this poem could be a good excuse for starting that tradition.

TAKEAWAY

Look for the bare necessities. The simple bare necessities. Forget about your worries and your strife.

> *"A righteous man who walks in his integrity—*
> *how blessed are his sons after him."*
>
> —Proverbs 20:7 NASB

A Son Needs His Dad…

To Bestow Quiet Courage

Some might say the opposite of *courage* is *fear*. They would not be wrong. But I suggest the opposite of *courage* may very well be *discourage*. You can see how courage and discouragement are at opposite ends of the personality spectrum. A man of courage pursues great challenges and noble causes. In the end, there's a high potential for grand achievement. But a man filled with discouragement doesn't bother. He has lost every battle before it has even begun.

I know you. Like me, you're a dad who wants your son to grow to be a man of great courage. Then why do we exasperate, belittle, and mock our boys? The Bible is clear: "Fathers, do not embitter your children, or they will become discouraged" (Colossians 3:21).

I hate this verse. I hate to think about fathers who leave their children with a bitter taste—joyless, resentful. I hate the idea of a son—a young life with great potential—giving up and just not caring anymore. I hate to consider that I may have brought a measure of discouragement to one or more of my children.

It's pretty easy to do. We slide a clever sarcastic remark across the dinner table. We chastise our kids for behavior we've been modeling for years. We set expectations that are beyond their capabilities or far different from their hopes and dreams. We make a correction and then make it again, again, and again without giving them time to process it. We run them down or embarrass them in front of their friends.

And here's a thoughtless response of which I've been guilty. Through extra effort and determination one of my sons would make an improvement in a field of study, athletics, creative arts, or other worthwhile pursuit. Instead of congratulating or celebrating, I would give off a vibe or even use words that say, "It's about time" or "Of course—I would expect nothing less." What a buzz kill.

79

Often, when we're trying to do the right thing as fathers is exactly when we push too hard or say too much.

It might even be possible that we're jealous of our sons. Of course, we want them to succeed. We want them to reach for the stars, and we rejoice in their achievements that go beyond anything we ever dreamed of doing. In sports. In business. In romance. In fame and glory. In those moments that should be celebratory, some fathers will look at their own life and see too many lost opportunities. Without thinking, we grab that chance to dash the celebration with snide words that belittle and discredit our own flesh and blood. What fools we are when we allow the male ego to steal joy from those we love. That's Satan working overtime.

May I suggest we choose now to always respond to our sons in ways that do not discourage, but give courage? When he triumphs, come alongside him. When he comes up just short, come alongside him. When he fails dramatically, come alongside him. In every case, dispense only quiet words of courage. *"I'm proud of you." "I know it's not the outcome you wanted, but what a great season." "Thank you, son. I wouldn't trade this moment for anything."* Or maybe don't say anything. It's surprising how often simply your presence is enough.

Then, when he's earned his own spot in the spotlight and finds himself listening humbly to a standing ovation in his honor, he'll pause, clear his throat, and give credit to the old man sitting off to one side. That's you, Dad. Well done.

TAKEAWAY

As with so many biblical admonitions, it's helpful to look at Colossians 3:21 from a reverse angle. Allow me to paraphrase. "Dads, speak encouragement to kids and allow them to chase their dreams and they will become courageous and empowered."

> *"You don't raise heroes, you raise sons. And if you treat them like sons, they'll turn out to be heroes, even if it's just in your own eyes."*
>
> —WALTER M. SCHIRRA SR.

A Son Needs His Dad...

To Remember What It Was Like

B e careful with this idea. The goal is not to relive your youth (like some silly Disney movie in which dads and teens switch roles).

But it's a really good idea—once in a while—to remember what it was like when you were a young buck. So, literally, grab a yellow pad or open a new Word document and list ten things you did or thought about doing when you were the age your son is right now. To get in the right frame of mind, do mental associations with the stuff you know for sure:

Who was your best friend? What kind of stuff did you guys do?

Who were your teachers? What projects and extracurriculars do you associate with that school or classroom experience?

What did your room look like? What was on the shelves? On the walls? Under the bed? Hidden from your parents?

How old were your siblings? Did you look up to them? Or down on them? Were they bullies or brats?

Favorite TV shows? Books? Movies? Video games? Fashions? A web search can tell you what was popular that year.

What teams were you on? Were you the hero or did you ride the bench? Any hard-earned trophies? (Don't count "participation" trophies.)

What gifts did you get for your birthday or Christmas that year?

Pull out a school yearbook. Or unpack one of those memory boxes in your parents' basement or attic. (Don't get angry if some of your old memorabilia found its way to the dumpster.)

Maybe ask your mom what you were like. Or even track down your old classmates and stir up some memories.

This exercise is not for you. It's so that you can be a better father to your son. Take a few days and daydream about your youth. Again, especially when you were the same age he is now. What was going through your puny head? What did you dream about? Did any of those dreams come true? What were you scared of? Did any of those fears come true?

Don't reveal your list to your son right away. Maybe go over it with your bride so that she can better know you and know your son. Before you share that list with your son, look at it one more time through his eyes. There may be some choices or mistakes you made that you don't want him to know about. That's possible. But maybe the best way to keep him from making those same mistakes is to let him know about your regrets. That's a pretty powerful parenting strategy.

You may be afraid he'll use your past to justify his actions today, but just the opposite can be true. A smart kid will see your sincerity, appreciate your perspective, and maybe even seek out your advice as he works through his own choices.

Having trouble stirring up those memories? Maybe I can help: Were you a hippie? A punk rocker? Did you disco in the 1970s? Did you break-dance in the '80s? Did you vogue or grind in the 1990s? Did you get a Walkman for Christmas? A boom box? Did you have one of the first Macintosh computers? Did you skateboard or Rollerblade? What was your first car? A used Gremlin? Pinto? AMC Pacer? Did your parents drive a station wagon, minivan, or SUV? Did you watch those terrible sitcoms like *Three's Company, Family Ties,* and *Facts of Life*? Did you own light-up sneakers, a jean jacket, Ray-Ban sunglasses, or platform shoes? Did you waste hours playing Super Mario Brothers or Pac-Man? Did you have a mullet, a rattail, a Mohawk, or huge sideburns? What historic events mark your youth? Watergate? The fall of the Berlin Wall? Mount St. Helens? Chernobyl? The space shuttle *Challenger* disintegrating 73 seconds after launch? The Columbine shooting? September 11?

Those are more than memories. Those are points of connection to the next generation. If you mention some of this stuff, are you afraid your son will roll his eyes? That's the idea! That gives you total permission to roll your eyes and groan at some of his choices today.

TAKEAWAY

In your youth, remember being amused by stories told by your parents or your aunts and uncles? There's something weirdly provocative about considering what your mom and dad were like when they were your age. Take advantage of that curiosity to connect with your kids.

> *"Encourage the young men to be self-controlled. In everything set them an example by doing what is good. In your teaching show integrity, seriousness and soundness of speech that cannot be condemned, so that those who oppose you may be ashamed because they have nothing bad to say about us."*
>
> —Titus 2:6-8

A Son Needs His Dad...

To Follow Through on Punishments

Wen you admonish your son, please follow through.

You've seen this happen at a park, restaurant, waiting room, or grocery store. A small child is doing something repetitive and irritating. His father says, "Stop." The kid doesn't. The father exhales and repeats, "Stop. I'm telling you to stop." The kid slows his irritating behavior momentarily, but doesn't really stop. The father exhales again and then makes a frowny face at the kid. (Which, by the way, is not a punishment.) Then, the father notices you, shrugs his shoulders, exhales again, and says, "Kids. What can you do?"

Wisely, you don't say a word. You know it would only end badly. But what you want to say is:

"What can you do? I'll tell you what to do. When you tell your kid to stop, make sure he stops. If you're not going to follow through, don't bother giving him any instructions. If you didn't know, your kid desperately needs you to say what you mean and mean what you say. If he doesn't listen to you now when he's not even in school yet, what makes you think you'll have any authority in ten years when his decisions really matter? Dude, you're a stinking wimp. Your son needs a man with integrity, courage, and authority. Someone he can trust. You sad-excuse-for-a-father are the launchpad from which your son is going to blast off into the world. But since you stand for nothing, you are guaranteeing that he is going to explode, implode, or just topple over into the mud and muck of the pitiful example you are setting for him. And by the way, my son, who has a dad with his act together, will end up picking up the pieces and paying for the disastrous life you have given to your son."

Well, that may be a bit harsh, but I'm only repeating what you're thinking.

Just to be clear, here are a few more examples of how a dad should follow through on his promises.

"If you leave another empty pop can on the coffee table, you will not have another can for two weeks."

"If you disrespect your mother again, you're on kitchen duty for a week."

"If you miss the school bus again, no video games for a week."

"If you chew with your mouth open again, we're canceling the family vacation to France with the nonrefundable airplane tickets."

That last ridiculous example was included to make a couple of points. Don't punish too severely for involuntary behavior like elbows on the table, sleeping during a church service, or forgetting to turn lights off. Also, don't assign punishments that penalize the rest of the family or would never be executed. In the moment, it's not easy to think ahead, but any decrees you make should come with reasonable and enforceable penalties for infractions that are specific and willful.

Punishments and consequences should be a training tool, not a horrifying sword of justice dangling over the neck of your son who is mostly a pretty good kid. Also, like a prisoner earning time off for good behavior, there should always be room for a reprieve. When you end a punishment a few days early, go ahead and underscore how your generous nature has prevailed. Explain how since your son has learned his lesson, you have been inspired to offer him a measure of grace. You could even point out how forgiving his transgressions has precedent in the Bible.

Finally, like so many lessons for dads, there's a flip side to all of this. You need to follow through on punishments…and promises.

Near the end of the school year, you might casually say, "Hey guys, let's try out that new water park this summer." To your kids, that's a promise and needs to be kept. No excuses. If it's a problem following through on your word, then maybe try considering your words more carefully. I speak from experience.

You see, Dad, if you do a thorough job following through on your promises, you may begin to see fewer and fewer instances in which you need to follow through on your punishments.

=== TAKEAWAY ===

Your word has exceptional value. Until you break it. Then it doesn't.

"Those that are most slow in making a promise
are the most faithful in the performance of it."

—Jean-Jacques Rousseau (1712–1778)

A Son Needs His Dad…

To Put a Positive Spin on Video Games

Maybe we got lucky. Somehow my sons' lives were not ruled by video games. Sure, they were busy with sports and other activities. Plus the four brothers always had someone looking to throw around a football, baseball, basketball, or Frisbee. But from what I hear, in many communities it's an epidemic.

We did have a couple of rules. House rule #1: Mom had to approve all games. And while I might have said okay to some of the mid-range violent games, Mom didn't. And the boys knew that. House rule #2: they couldn't play alone. So, even if they were inside blasting aliens or playing Madden NFL Football, they were at least interacting with another human in the same room.

I asked a couple of friends with boys a little younger than mine how they are dealing with the issue right now. Tim confirmed that "threats, yelling, pleading, and criticism" do not work. Their house rules required his two sons to ask permission to play and then set the kitchen timer for 45 minutes. But that mostly just led to shouts of "Did you HEAR the timer?"

Tim and his wife, Debbie, did do a "fair amount of praying" about the issue. Lo and behold, that did work. Their oldest son increased his interest in real-life athletics, which cut down on gaming. Their younger son saw his occasional interest in video games evolve into a true passion for video production. Tim invested in some editing and special-effects software, and the young man is pursuing a career in video postproduction.

Terry has four sons. He grew up playing Pong, Nintendo, and Sega and readily acknowledges the allure and potential waste of time. He also confirms that Pong skills do not translate to the sophisticated games of today. Terry and his wife, Jenny, faced the issue head-on. They picked up some gaming magazines and researched video games that had high rankings for quality, playability, and fun, but low violence and sexual content. Terry said you'd be "surprised at the number of games with high ratings that do not carry a Mature or even Teen rating."

Terry also insists that video-game time always include brother-to-brother interaction. He even suggests a series of games called "Little Big Planet." He said, "For me to see a 16-year-old brother working alongside and supporting his 9-year-old brother is pretty cool." Families with fewer kids may need to flex on this rule or frequently engage a friend or even Dad in friendly competition. (Dad, expect to lose.)

Other ground rules Terry and Jenny set up: No video games during the school week. No exceptions. On weekends, time is allotted based on their family schedule. The need to pull the plug completely never really happens. Terry listed many specific alternatives that naturally get the boys off the gaming systems: touch football, Ping-Pong, basketball, beanbag toss, badminton, street hockey, Frisbee golf, or jumping on their bikes to hit the tennis courts or grab a Slurpee at 7-Eleven. When the boys were younger, Mom and Dad would come up with things to do other than video games—now the boys take it upon themselves.

I'm going to give Terry credit for the best insight imaginable when it comes to the tough task of pulling your son away from any activity that has begun to take over his life. He reminds us that "if you really want to take the video controller out of your kid's hands...replace it with you! Time with Dad is what kids want most. Even older kids will jump at the chance."

Thanks, Tim. Thanks, Terry. That's more proof that men should get together regularly and share ideas on how to be the dads God is calling us to be.

TAKEAWAY

Invest a little effort, a little creativity, and a little prayer, and maybe our sons aren't going to turn into zoned-out, brain-dead zombies after all.

"I recently learned something quite interesting about video games. Many young people have developed incredible hand, eye, and brain coordination in playing these games. The air force believes these kids will be our outstanding pilots should they fly our jets."
—RONALD REAGAN (1911–2004)

A Son Needs His Dad...

To Stir the Conversation Pot

After my dad died, I realized all the conversations I had not had with him. On the one hand, that seems silly. He and I had a great relationship. He was a busy guy, an elementary-school principal for more than 30 years with all kinds of meetings and obligations. But I never felt shortchanged or neglected. His discipline was fair. When I needed him, he was there. Especially in the last several years of his life, we had good conversations. I never felt shut out.

But since his death just a few years ago, questions regularly come to mind that now will never be answered.

"If you hadn't gone into teaching, what other career path might you have taken?"

"What did you think about Supreme Court decisions passed while you were raising a family? Banning school prayer? Roe v. Wade?"

"Did your dad go to your football games?"

"Did your dad play catch with you?"

"Did you ever think about changing churches?"

"What was the toughest thing about Mom's radical double mastectomy?"

"Why did our family trips pretty much avoid crowds and big cities?"

"Any regrets? Things that never got checked off your bucket list?"

Part of me always worried about disappointing my dad. He never really set benchmarks or expectations, so part of me always wondered if he was proud of me. Did his two sons and two daughters ever let him down? My first few books were published before he died and I know he enjoyed giving copies to people. I made sure he had a good supply.

One question I had that may seem trivial was whether he was disappointed that I had never found satisfaction in sitting in a rowboat for hours at a time waiting for a bluegill, crappie, or northern pike to tug on my line.

My dad enjoyed that. At least I think he did. For decades, every August the Payleitner family went "up north" with grandparents and extended family to share in the traditions of catching, cleaning, and talking about fish. I didn't get it. I absolutely enjoyed the time with my dad and brother, and I recall specific conversations and cherish the memories. But for this boy, an hour on the water would have been enough. Four hours, not so much. Out of my teens, I never pursued the sport.

A few months after Dad died, I asked my mom if it made him sad that I had never become an avid fisherman. She looked at me quizzically and confirmed that it was never an issue. Clearly, Dad had shared 50 years of experiences with me. Fishing was just one of many. The fact that I didn't share that one hobby was hardly a concern. I was glad to hear it.

Still, I wish I had asked Dad that question.

But conversation is a two-way street. As a son, I may not have asked those questions. But as a dad, I need to make sure that my own sons are comfortable asking any question at any time. Sometimes that means me asking a few open-ended questions. Sometimes that means asking an opinion on a controversial subject.

Then be ready. When you stir the conversation pot the result may be an opinion that differs from yours. Perhaps one you don't want to hear. Take care not to come across so pigheaded that you don't listen to their side and their arguments. Don't be afraid to take a stand, especially on issues of morality, integrity, and core theological truths, but always keep the door open to more dialogue.

In many ways, verbal sparring with your boys is more important than any physical activities you may ever do with them. A healthy debate between a father and son can be very rewarding for both sides. Especially as they head into adulthood.

TAKEAWAY

Is there anything left unsaid between you and your father? Something minuscule in importance? Something significant? Maybe...maybe, call him today.

"Many men go fishing their entire lives without knowing it is not fish they are after."
—HENRY DAVID THOREAU (1817–1862)

A Son Needs His Dad…

To Sign Him Up for a Traveling Sports Team

Get your son involved in traveling baseball, soccer, track, volleyball, wrestling, gymnastics, ice skating, hockey, basketball, lacrosse, judo, fencing, golf, archery, and so on.

Are you surprised by such a recommendation? You might be if you've been listening to the opinions of some youth pastors and other church leaders. Traveling sports are getting an unjustifiable bad rap these days from the pulpit. We're told that traveling sports invariably become an idol or obsession. We're told that parents who allow their children to participate in traveling sports are pushing them too hard. We're told that traveling sports are a distraction from Sunday-morning church. I guess that's all possible. But I also think it's being regretfully shortsighted.

If your son shows some above average talent in a sport—or really any activity—I recommend you keep your eyes open for a chance to expose those talents to the next level of competition. There's a good chance he's already thinking about it. His pals are signing up and asking him to join. In many parts of the country, coaches and leagues actively publicize their programs and recruit for members. It's big business, and many families get caught up in the frenzy, so prepare yourself to be a voice of reason. But that's all part of the learning curve when raising a son who has legitimate talent and sincere desire.

The benefits of having a child over 12 on a traveling team with high expectations and an occasional overnight tournament are incalculable. What will they learn? Perseverance, self-denial, hard work, sacrifice, dedication, time management, and respect for authority. Plus, teamwork, making tough choices, leadership, winning with humility, and losing with grace. All under your watchful eye.

Perhaps the greatest bonus is the chance to spend one-on-one time together in the car, between events, and sharing a motel room. Remember how your son would eagerly drop everything to spend time with you? That attitude doesn't last forever. Now that he's older, you need a strategy for staying in his life. The intense and mandatory schedule of a traveling sports team requires both of you to make time in your calendar for each other. Those sometimes grueling trips served as rites of passage for all my kids.

Did we miss some Sunday-morning services at our home church? Of course. We talked about that choice. We talked about legalism and grace. Together we acknowledged and honored the Sabbath. My kids also sacrificed some youth group activities. But they remained committed to their teams, often seeing them as a mission field. They modeled the Christian life on and off the field. They boldly stood their ground with unchurched teammates, something they never would have experienced sitting in a church rec room.

Our son Max was no angel, but he proved to have a positive influence on his teammates. Years later, one mother told us that "When my son went out, I always knew that if Max was along, he wouldn't get in any trouble."

The wins and losses have blurred with time. But the investment of time and money in traveling sports was worth every nickel and every hour.

TAKEAWAY

Don't force your son into sports. But if he commits, you commit 110 percent. Following your good judgment, the same probably applies to debate, speech, Science Olympiads, mock trial, chess, jazz band, Model UN, robotics, automotive design, and a myriad of other competitive activities up through his high-school years.

"Sports don't build character; they reveal it."
—JOHN WOODEN (1910–2010)

A Son Needs His Dad...

To Respond to Blunders with "Did You Learn Anything?"

I'm tight with the guys at Fathers.com. That's the website of the National Center for Fathering in Kansas City, founded by Ken Canfield and now headed up by Carey Casey. More than 20 years ago, I helped launch and I still help script their daily three-minute radio broadcast for dads heard on more than 400 stations. It's one of the great privileges of my life.

There's more about that great organization in the back of this book, but one of the coolest things they do is sponsor essay contests around the country on the topic "What My Father Means to Me." Kids of all ages write short essays about their fathers, stepfathers, grandfathers, and father figures. Some of the winning entries are posted online, and you can't read them without coming away inspired with fresh fathering ideas and a solid reminder of the importance of being a dad.

A high-school senior named Eric wrote a recent entry with all kinds of lessons for dads. His essay titled "Did You Learn Anything?" is based on a phrase Eric's father used often. Here's an excerpt:

> This quote was quickly thrown out with a smile every time I did something wrong in childhood. My dad has always been more concerned about me learning from past experiences than [punishing me] when I actually goof up. I remember in grade school when I ran our riding lawn mower into a tree because I had been texting. Instead of a lengthy lecture, my dad just smiled and threw out the old faithful quote: "Did you learn anything?" Needless to say, I have not run my car into a tree because I was texting.

Good stuff, right? Well, let me unpack a few thoughts inspired by Eric and his father.

First, that four-word phrase is a much better response than most dads typically make when a child messes up. Too often we feel like we have to make him feel bad or show him who's boss. But if we really have his best interests in mind, we'll take the longer view. When something unfortunate happens, let's maximize the chances that he'll learn something he can use later in life. Instead of a lecture, Eric's father allowed the lesson to speak for itself.

Even more interesting is the connection that Eric made on his own regarding the huge problem of texting while driving. If Eric's dad had delivered a ten-minute rant on "Why aren't you more responsible?" there's a high probability Eric would have shut down and never applied that lesson learned on a riding mower to his behavior behind the wheel of a car.

Also worth noting, Eric's father always includes a smile when he asks, "Did you learn anything?" That's critical for building bridges and delivering life lessons. When our sons mess up, too often we make our anger and disappointment the main issue. They will inevitably respond with their own high emotions of embarrassment, shame, anger, or denial. No lessons learned. No one wins.

A couple other thoughts always come to me when I read these "What My Father Means to Me" essays. Like most dads, I wonder what my own kids would write. And I also think about how world-changing it would be if dads everywhere began to share their fathering secrets with each other. Eric's dad somehow came up with that very helpful four-word phrase. His son passed it on to the National Center for Fathering. They passed it on to me. And now I'm passing it on to you.

Will you use it? Will you pass it on?

TAKEAWAY

Dad, try it next time your child messes up. Don't lecture, put a smile on your face, and ask, "Did you learn anything?"

> *"We know that God causes everything to work*
> *together for the good of those who love God and*
> *are called according to his purpose for them."*
> —ROMANS 8:28 NLT

A SON NEEDS HIS DAD…

To Train Him to Trust Wisely

For the first few years of your son's life, he believes the world revolves around him. And in many ways it does.

When he's hungry, wet, or scared, someone (typically Mom or Dad) feeds him, changes his diaper, and calms his fears. Especially in that first year of life, please don't worry about spoiling him. What you're doing is teaching him to trust you. You're proving that he can count on you. You're the one who is going to supply all his needs.

In a few short years, you are not going to be the center of his universe. He's going to leave the safe harbor of Mom and Dad's world and begin to construct his own world. That's a good thing. If you've given him a proper foundation, as the Bible instructs, he's going to stay the course.

> *Train up a child in the way he should go, even when he is old he will not depart from it (Proverbs 22:6 NASB).*

Trust is a virtue. It's closely related to faith and self-confidence. At some point, every Christian needs to say, "I don't see God. But I see God's creation, I see God working in the lives of his people, and I trust his plan for my life."

To get to that point, your son will need a dose of curiosity and a pinch of skepticism. He's got to own his own faith. He needs to take the lessons you've taught him and apply them to real life. At some point you can no longer use the lazy parent's command: "Because I said so." When you want him to do something or take a stand, you have to be able to say, "This is the right thing to do because it has value and there are moral convictions behind it based on God's character."

Eventually the goal is for your son to move on and out with a set of personal convictions he can defend. A young man who has learned to trust will carry the kind of fresh optimism and hope that we need more of in this world.

But notice, I didn't say gullible. Being gullible comes with its own set of problems.

Someone who trusts without thinking and follows with eyes closed will be taken in by the latest trends, swayed by false gods, or fooled by con artists. I'm amazed by how many intelligent adults are so easily sucked into the world of Ponzi schemes, multilevel marketing, fad diets, fraudulent medical treatments, and other deceptions and half-truths. It seems that Christians are especially susceptible. Maybe that's because many Christians are taught to trust, but never given any real tools of discernment.

On the trust spectrum, you want your son to fall right in the middle. On one end is the lazy-brained goof who is easily bamboozled. It's not that he trusts too much, it's that he doesn't think for himself and has nowhere else to turn.

Way off on the other end of the trust spectrum is a cynical pessimist that expects the worst from the world. He's the guy who believes in every conspiracy theory out there and probably thinks the church is just a racket for conning money from the ignorant masses.

In the middle, your son will carefully consider his options and make wise choices. The purpose of this chapter is to remind you and him that he doesn't have to do it alone.

Or course, he has your example and teaching as a foundation.

> *You must remain faithful to the things you have been taught. You know they are true, for you know you can trust those who taught you (2 Timothy 3:14 NLT).*

He needs also to surround himself with men and women who bring their own experience and proven integrity.

> *Plans fail for lack of counsel, but with many advisers they succeed (Proverbs 15:22).*

Without hesitation, he can ask God any question anytime and anyplace.

> *If any of you lacks wisdom, you should ask God, who gives generously to all without finding fault, and it will be given to you (James 1:5).*

The truths of the Bible will never let him down.

> *All Scripture is God-breathed and is useful for teaching, rebuking, correcting and training in righteousness, so that the servant of God may be thoroughly equipped for every good work (2 Timothy 3:16-17).*

And when the voices of the world begin to seduce him with lust, greed, power, and fame, let him know that's a pretty good clue to run the other way.

> *Do not conform to the pattern of this world, but be transformed by the renewing of your mind. Then you will be able to test and approve what God's will is—his good, pleasing and perfect will (Romans 12:2).*

But remember, Dad, it all starts with you. You are the first person who really teaches him to trust. Moms cuddle close and coo sweetly. Dad is the one who holds him high off the floor, but would never let him fall. Dad is the one who leaves for hours or even days at a time, but always comes back. Dad is the one who wrestles and growls, but stops before it gets really scary. Dad is the one who makes promises about the future and keeps his word every time. A boy can trust his dad. And trust is the foundation of faith.

TAKEAWAY

The goal is for your son to begin life trusting you and grow into a relationship in which he trusts God.

> *"We're never so vulnerable than when we trust someone—but paradoxically, if we cannot trust, neither can we find love or joy."*
>
> —WALTER ANDERSON (1944–)

A Son Needs His Dad...

To Help Him Not Choke in the Clutch

My baseball career peaked the summer I turned ten. For some reason, our park district had nine- and ten-year-old boys playing with a ten-inch softball. Pitchers threw underhand windmill-style. My baseball savvy, jetlike speed, and fearless composure at the plate made me the best dang player on the Tigers. My dad coached and I often played short center. I made at least a half dozen unassisted double plays by catching short fly balls and stepping on second base when a less competent runner forgot to tag up. It was a blast.

The following year, I moved up to the next level, which meant facing hardballs pitched overhand by boys who couldn't always find the plate. My belief in myself was shaken. From the start, the new coach was not impressed. So the summer I turned 11, I rode the bench and got a total of one hit. The next year my dad conveniently forgot to sign me up for baseball. Thinking back, I'm pretty sure he didn't want to go through the agony of watching his son fail.

The next few summers of my fading youth, my brother and I played hours and hours of pickup games with neighborhood boys in the field next door. A row of bicycles served as a backstop. Carpet squares were bases. It reignited my love for the sport. But I never wore a baseball uniform again. And somewhere along the way, I lost a little confidence in my athletic ability.

In most of my sports endeavors after that, it seemed like when the game didn't matter or we were just playing for fun, I held my own. I stayed loose and made the plays. But in big games or late innings, I'd tense up and start thinking way too much about mechanics and strategy. In men's slow pitch, that big old softball would float down through the strike zone and I'd hit a pop-up to second. On the golf course, just playing for fun, I showed a little potential.

But trying to keep up with experienced golfers, my game got embarrassing. Even in high-school wrestling, I would do pretty well during the season, but misfire during tournaments.

In other words, when I felt pressure to step it up a notch, I got worse. Do they still call that "choking in the clutch"?

Well, all of that came as an unwelcome and slightly painful realization. Which honestly I did not want my boys to suffer. So I began brainwashing them. (Or maybe a better term is *suggesting an improved course of action*.) I'm not sure it worked, but their athletic careers all surpassed mine. So maybe my strategy is worth passing on to you, father to father.

Here's what I did. While watching a televised sporting event with any of my boys, sooner or later the announcers would talk about a player who either did or did not get the job done at a critical situation. For example, a place-kicker who confidently drills 50-yard field goals in the last seconds of games. A reliever who finishes the year with zero blown saves. A .230 career batter who hits .400 in the postseason to earn the nickname Mr. October. Conversely, there are just as many grim stories of running backs who fumble in overtime or the golfer who misses a three-foot putt in sudden death. How players respond in the clutch has become routine sports banter.

When the topic came up with Alec, Randall, Max, or Isaac, I would share my own woeful tale of losing my edge and caving under pressure. But then quickly add, "That's one of the reasons I love watching you play. You get better under pressure. I've seen it. At key situations, somehow you turn your game up a notch." And then I'd leave it at that.

Was I lying? Not at all. My perception has always been that my boys were superior athletes. Really, all I was doing was helping them imagine a successful outcome when facing a challenge in the future. Doesn't that describe the most important thing a father can do for a son? Give them hope for the future?

This specific example may not apply to you and your son. But it's a good reminder that some of the most valuable tools you have as a father are stories of your past successes and failures. Just make sure your successes aren't so glorious that your son can't possibly ever live up to them. And make sure you talk about your failures as a chance to grow and learn. Pass them on with the goal that he won't make the same mistakes you made.

And what do you know? You no longer have to carry any regrets because every win and loss you experienced has made you the awesome dad you are today.

━━━━━━━━━━━━━━ **TAKEAWAY** ━━━━━━━━━━━━━━

Certain words from a father echo for decades in the memory of a son. The problem, of course, is that you don't know which ones. Whenever possible choose words that deliver hope, not despair.

> *"A righteous man falls seven times, and rises again,*
> *but the wicked stumble in time of calamity."*
>
> —PROVERBS 24:16 NASB

A Son Needs His Dad...

To Expose Him to the Dark Side

R ita likes to hold babies. Which works out well because babies like to be held.

While working on this manuscript, our first grandson was born, so my bride is getting lots of satisfaction in that area these days. Young Jackson David Payleitner is both cuddly and amusing.

There was a time when we had lots of growing kids in our home, but not very many babies. So Rita took that deep desire and put it to very good use. Over a period of several years, we had ten foster babies in our home.

One of the challenges of the child-welfare and foster-care system is that it's difficult to remove children from abusive environments. The legal system works very slowly and there are just too many hurting kids. Every case requires thorough investigation, stacks of documentation, and judicial review. All of which takes months. Except in the case of babies born with cocaine in their system. If the birth mother has a history of drug use or the infant shows specific symptoms, newborns in our state are tested for cocaine exposure. If they test positive, that means mom was doing crack and endangering her unborn child. And that child is automatically placed in the welfare system.

Not all of them, but some of the newborns that came to stay with us were essentially recovering addicts. I will never forget my son Max holding one of those precious babies while she was experiencing severe withdrawal tremors. You have to understand this was right around the time Max was an all-conference fullback, a state-qualifying wrestler, and starting catcher for the baseball team that placed fourth in the state. He was a tough kid with a high threshold for pain. But watching that baby shake uncontrollably because of a birth mother's selfish choices broke Max's heart and made him a little angry. "How could a mother do this to her baby?" he demanded.

Max was never on a path to drug or alcohol abuse, but you can imagine how holding that helpless baby in the throes of a seizure was a wake-up call for the hopelessness and waste of life that comes from addictive behaviors. What started as Rita's love for babies became a life lesson for every member of the Payleitner family.

And so it is with every family. If you live in a private world and only allow people like you to enter, you'll live in a sort of denial. We need to recognize that the world is broken. And that has repercussions for all of us. One of the Gospel writers well explains why people continue to hang on to their sinful condition. They've been living in the dark so long, they fear the light.

> *God's light came into the world, but people loved the darkness more than the light, for their actions were evil. All who do evil hate the light and refuse to go near it for fear their sins will be exposed. But those who do what is right come to the light so others can see that they are doing what God wants (John 3:19-21 NLT).*

When those cocaine-exposed babies came into our home, they brought a reluctant acceptance of reality. It was a truth my family needed to acknowledge. Beyond volunteering for foster care, there are many ways you can make your family aware of the desperate condition of our world. Going on short-term mission trips. Reading biographies of missionaries and martyrs. Volunteering at prisons, soup kitchens, and homeless shelters. Opening your home to international refugees. Providing diapers and baby clothes to pregnancy-resource centers. Or it may be as simple as creating a home environment where your children invite their friends so they can feel safe and loved right in their own community.

You'll discover that even as you wisely expose your family to the darkness of our world, you're also shining light into those dark corners. God will use any light you provide to guide hurting people to a relationship with him.

Two final notes on this chapter:

Love is a powerful force. I saw my wife and kids love that cocaine residue right out of those babies. The boys and girls we've been able to keep track of over the years are doing very, very well.

Max learned how to hold newborns, change diapers, and make babies laugh while he was still in high school. And he's doing an even better job today with his son, Jackson.

TAKEAWAY

When one member of your family has an aching need motivated by love—to hold babies, to feed the hungry, to volunteer at Special Olympics, to pick up trash on the highway, to build homes in Appalachia—encourage the rest of the family to be cheerleaders and maybe even involved partners in that work. It multiplies the impact. And brings your family closer together.

"Three things will last forever—faith, hope, and love—and the greatest of these is love."

—1 Corinthians 13:13 NLT

A Son Needs His Dad...

To Really Love His Mom

If you are not married to your son's mother, you have to work overtime to respect her, cooperate with her, and do everything in your power to help her be the best mom she can be. Your son needs his mom as much as he needs you. So no debate and no excuses. Okay?

Let's move on, because that's not what this chapter is about.

This chapter is about being an awesome husband so that your son will know how to be an awesome husband himself someday. In two-and-a-half pages, I'm going to save you $12.99 and summarize my book *52 Things Wives Need from Their Husbands*. Ready?

Cherish her. Women need to feel loved and honored. Even if they are strong and independent, they need a man who would die for them.

Don't say stuff you already know will tick her off. No one knows your wife like you. You know her fears and her trigger points. Every time you walk in the door, you could start an argument. So don't always say what you're thinking. Instead, say the opposite. And tell her you are glad you married her.

Don't keep score. Too many guys think that they are making tremendous sacrifices for their brides. But if you really keep track, you would see that she puts more effort into the marriage and family than you. Remember Genesis 2:24, which describes marriage as two becoming one flesh? Most guys think, *If I give her what she likes, she'll give me what I like.* That's a recipe for disaster. You should be thinking, *If I give her what she likes, it gives me joy as well.*

Really listen. When she wants to talk, put down the paper and turn off the radio. Don't eat dinner at sports bars. The game on the big screen behind your wife will get all your attention. Oh yeah, if she says something and you missed it, admit it.

Fall on the grenade. Expect to apologize more often than she does. Three reasons: 1) As risk takers, we men mess up more. 2) As men, we know how to take one for the team. 3) Women are the gatekeeper when it comes to romance. When we finally do apologize, the real question is "What took us so long?"

Practice nagging prevention. Instead of flopping on the sofa when you come home, say, "Is there anything that needs doing around here?" If she says "Yes," do it. But most of the time, she'll say "No, dear." Suddenly there's nothing to nag about.

Be the pastor in your home. Here's the formula: *do…model…teach*. Here are some examples: Pray…let your family see you pray…encourage them to pray. Tell the truth…let your family hear you speak only truth…encourage them to be truthful. Read the Bible…let your family see…encourage them to read the Bible. Volunteer…let them see you volunteer…invite them to join you. Your wife wants and needs you to lead your family spiritually. *Do. Model. Teach.*

Lust for your bride. Choose to only have eyes for her. Love her every wrinkle, every gray hair, every extra pound. Flee pornography. Instead see only her. Her smile. Her eyes. Her hidden beauty. Remove all competition. Your bride is the most beautiful woman in the world.

Rage not. Proverbs 14:29 says, "Whoever is patient has great understanding, but one who is quick-tempered displays folly." Gentlemen, you rage, you lose. Every time.

Get the job done in the bedroom. Talk about it. Ask her what she wants. Be creative. But not too creative.

Stay married. Every time I speak, guys come up to me who say they want to be great dads, but they live across town or across the state from their kids. Instead of thinking up reasons to divorce, spend that same effort looking for reasons to stay married.

Surprise her with gifts. Come on, dude. You know she loves flowers and little gifts. It's so easy, but we don't do it. And it doesn't have to be expensive. It really is the thought that counts.

Anticipate the seasons of marriage. She will make mistakes. You will disappoint her. Kids will exhaust both of you. Kids will exhilarate both of you. Friends will fail you. Jobs will be lost. Cash will be tight. Illness will come. Let all of life—the good and bad—bring the two of you closer together. Trust love.

I'm afraid that a high percentage of young men these days don't see the value of marriage or want to take on such a responsibility. They can't imagine making a lifelong commitment. Or worse, they think it's no big deal and don't take marriage seriously.

Traditional marriage is the building block of family, community, and nation. The eyes of a million young people are watching to see if marriage is worth saving.

TAKEAWAY

Great marriages are worth the effort. Can I say that my four sons must have had a positive experience watching Rita and me? In the last five years, we've welcomed four magnificent daughters-in-law to our family. Even better, Grandma Rita is more beautiful than ever.

"In a good marriage each is the other's better half."
—ALFRED HITCHCOCK (1889–1980)

A Son Needs His Dad...

To Cut Him a Few Deals

Rita and I never did this, but it might not be a bad strategy for encouraging better grades. When your son's report card comes home, each "B" earns an Alexander Hamilton and each "A" earns an Andrew Jackson. Hey, whatever it takes, right? You would hope the deep gratification of gaining knowledge would propel your boy to strive for excellence in school, but—surprise, surprise—sometimes it doesn't work that way.

I've heard of other deals from other dads:

My pastor, Jim Nicodem, confessed from the pulpit that over the summer he paid his kids for each book they read and briefly summarized. He said it was one of the best investments he ever made. In his book *Man Alive*, Patrick Morley writes (on page 135) that he paid his kids to read the Bible. Even better.

One dad was tired of buying sports equipment and musical instruments that were never used, so he made deals like this: "Son, if you master the acoustic guitar (or reach a certain level of competence), then I'll buy you an electric guitar." "If you stick with baseball this year using your cheap aluminum bat, then I'll spring for the double-wall titanium bat next year."

My own father made a deal, not with his kids, but with his 11 grandchildren. Ken Payleitner had learned to smoke during World War II when the military handed out packets of Lucky Strikes along with C-rations. He didn't want that nasty habit to be part of his legacy. Papa told each of his grandkids that if they graduated from high school without smoking, he or she would get a hundred bucks. That deal wound up costing him $1100.

I'll also never forget another deal my dad made with my son Alec when he was about six. For Christmas, Papa bought Alec a cheap harmonica and said, "Play me a song and I'll buy you the best one in the store." Later that afternoon, Alec surprised us all by playing a snappy rendition of "Jingle Bells."

Before the New Year, Papa took his grandson out for a pretty nice Hohner harmonica. Alec used that same instrument on stage more than a decade later.

My dad demonstrated one of the key principles of deal-making with kids. Keep your promise ASAP. In the adult world, we know that sometimes you have to wait for payments, contracts, rebates, and other deals. But a few days to a kid is an eternity. Sure, children need to learn patience. But when they're waiting on Dad to keep up his end of the bargain, don't make them wait. You'll have plenty of time to teach them patience when they're waiting on a deep-dish pizza, sitting in the pediatrician's waiting room, or driving to the Grand Canyon. Those things are out of your control. Besides, if you make a deal and forget about it, suddenly your deal-making has turned into promise-breaking, and any lesson has been lost.

A couple warnings. Some child psychologists are saying that rewarding kids with candy and dessert may be training them to associate success with pigging out. Because of that, your son's mom may panic about classrooms and clubs that give out candy once in a while. But really it's probably okay. Clearly, taking your son to DQ after he pulls a garden full of weeds is a pretty good idea.

Also, don't reward kids for doing what they should already be doing. If family rules dictate that he make his bed every morning, then that's not a rewardable activity. When it's his turn to mow the lawn or do the dishes, that's not making a deal. He's just pitching in as part of the family.

Let me finish this chapter with a few deals Rita and I did make with our kids.

- If they were in a high-school sport and earned academic all-conference recognition, Mom and Dad would pay for their car insurance.

- No TV time unless rooms were clean.

- Anytime we visited a Christian bookstore, I would buy any one item no questions asked: T-shirt, journal, music, video, poster, or even a book!

- For older teens and young adults home from college, if you wanted Sunday brunch, you had to get up and go to Sunday service.

Finally, this is a deal we worked out that has served our four boys well, especially after they got their driver's licenses. The deal came to be known as "Brother Bonding Time." All our sons had their own groups of friends, and still do. But for several years when they chose to do something just among themselves—two, three, or four at a time—somehow, Mom and Dad picked up all or most of the tab. That could be lunch, the driving range, the batting cage, bowling, or even going to the latest action-adventure movie. As part of the Payleitner men, sometimes I was invited. But that wasn't necessarily part of the deal. It was actually more fulfilling seeing three or four brothers climb into a car and head off on a bonding adventure together. Now that was a great deal.

TAKEAWAY

You're the dad. And what you say goes. But making a deal once in a while is an effective way to encourage behavior or just make sure a chore is accomplished. When you reward responsibility and positive activities, there's a real chance they become lifelong habits.

"Parents are not quite interested in justice,
they are interested in quiet."
—BILL COSBY (1937–)

A SON NEEDS HIS DAD...

To Defend Twenty-First-Century Chivalry

A s an advocate and cheerleader for dads, I receive quite a few stories from friends and colleagues. Here's one that had me regretting how I had let the changing culture *change me*. Things I instinctively wanted to do, I no longer did. Things I should have taught my sons, I didn't. See if you can relate.

The story begins with Dr. Samuel DeWitt Proctor on an elevator. The doors open and one of his female students steps on. The professor removes his hat. In his book *The Substance of Things Hoped For*, Dr. Proctor relates the following conversation:

> "Dr. Proctor," she said, "Why...did you take your hat off when I got in the elevator? You're living in the Victorian age." She laughed congenially.
>
> "If you'll get off the elevator with me for a moment, I'll tell you." At my stop, we both stepped off.
>
> "I'm not a Victorian," I said, "but some things stay in place from one generation to another, and certain manners stand for values that I hold dear. I believe that a society that ceases to respect women is on its way out. Women bear and raise our children, they are bound to them in early infancy; they need our support and security through this process. When we forget that, the keystone of family and home is lost. When we neglect and abuse women, the family falls apart and children are less well parented, and they fill up in the jails and are buried in early graves. I believe that respect for women is the linchpin of the family and the society.
>
> "Therefore, when you entered the elevator, I wanted you to have automatic, immediate, unqualified assurance that if the

elevator caught fire, I would help you out through the top first. If a strange man boarded and began to slap you around and tear your clothes off, he would have to kill me first. If the elevator broke down and stopped between floors, I would not leave you in there. If you fainted and slumped to the floor, I would stop everything and get you to a hospital.

"Now, it would take a lot of time to say all of that, so when I removed my hat, I meant all of the above."

I hope that student learned a lesson from that eloquent professor. From my experience, I doubt she did. As a young adult male in the 1980s working world, I quickly learned that certain women wanted no part of male chivalry. They were insulted if you opened the door for them, stood when they entered the room, or gave up your seat on the bus. Women who were supposedly seeking equality and respect often said nasty things or gave nasty looks. So I stopped doing it. And the world became a little colder and a little more selfish.

Looking back, I wish I had had the courage, convictions, and grace of Professor Proctor.

You and your son are not responsible to save the world from radical feminism or start quarrels with women who want to open their own doors. But you can certainly take a stand for mutual respect, tradition, and the art of being a gentleman.

Begin by teaching your son all the old-fashioned, supposedly Victorian rituals. That includes opening car doors, standing when appropriate, pulling out chairs, offering your coat when it's chilly, and maybe even taking off your hat in an elevator. In a busy office, on a factory floor, or in council chambers, your son will likely want to adapt his application of male chivalry. That's his choice, but he should at least know the rules. They no longer teach social etiquette and manners in school, so he's going to need your help.

As an aside: before your son's first date, young Romeo needs to be ready to meet the young lady's father and shake his hand, help her with her coat, open every door they approach, be prepared to pick up the tab, and walk her to her door at the end of the evening without expecting a kiss. He'll say, "I know all that, Dad." But tell him he has to hear you out anyway, especially if he's borrowing your car.

Finally, it's worth noting that Dr. Samuel DeWitt Proctor was a respected humanitarian, minister, and leader in the African-American civil-rights movement, and a friend and mentor of Dr. Martin Luther King Jr. The student on the elevator happened to be white. That certainly doesn't change the truth spoken by Dr. Proctor in that teachable moment. But it does remind us that your son will be working and living in a world that continues to change. Every generation faces new cultural realities. Your job, Dad, is to help him develop character traits that have eternal value. Things like chivalry, respect, integrity, self-control, compassion, generosity, humility, perseverance, and so many other virtues that have been lost over the years.

You might not have all these attributes mastered yourself, but as his father and mentor you should be ready to help your son rise above what the culture is saying and ask, "How is my relationship with God reflected in my choices and attitudes?"

You're the right man for the job, Dad. I tip my hat to you.

TAKEAWAY

As the world gets more selfish and more divided, maybe your son will grow into a leader who loves and unites. That possibility begins with you.

"Manners maketh man."
—WILLIAM OF WYKEHAM (1324–1404)

A SON NEEDS HIS DAD…
To Take the Generational Challenge

Here's a fascinating exercise. If you have the courage.

Take out a yellow legal pad or open a new Word doc and begin to list the attitudes, attributes, routines, and worldview you recall in your father. Things he did, the way he disciplined, how he interacted with others, hobbies, priorities, personality traits, and how he approached work, family, home, friends, neighbors, and religion.

It may be enlightening, heartwarming, difficult, or sad, but keep going until you have at least 20 or 30 character traits. Then, put pluses or minuses next to the qualities you consider to be positive traits and negative traits. Some traits on the list may be neither negative nor positive and that's okay.

Next draw a line through any of the qualities you don't see in yourself. If he was a gambler and that's not you, scratch it off the list. If he regularly visited inmates as part of a prison ministry and that's not your thing, scratch it off. Be honest.

Those things that remain just might be an eye-opening list of the heritage left to you from your father. For better or worse, you're still personally responsible for those qualities, but at least now you know where you learned them. Which leaves you with some real-life decisions. Are there any other qualities you need to cast aside and scratch off that list? I recommend you look again at the attributes marked with a minus sign. On the other hand, maybe there are a few things he did or attitudes he had that you may want to emulate.

Maybe you lie awake at night wondering if your father is or would be proud of you. Maybe he's the furthest thing from your mind. In any case, you can't deny that his influence on your life is significant. If you want to be the best you can be, the above exercise is worth the effort.

We could stop there, but this book is all about your impact on the next generation. So, the next logical step is to take your list and decide what you want your son to keep or cast away.

That puts an entirely new spin on the exercise, doesn't it? Thirty years from now, what response would you want your son to have from this kind of generational evaluation? He could think, *Look at all the rotten baggage my old man left me.* Or he could think, *My dad was always a pretty cool guy. I'm glad I turned out like him. Sure, he made some mistakes, but he never gave up and always tried to make things right.*

For better or worse, fathers make an indelible impression on the minds and hearts of the next generation of fathers. That includes all kinds of attitudes, opinions, virtues, and vices. Some good. Some not so good. So today, ask yourself and decide, *What am I going to hang onto? What am I going to cast aside?*

Hint: Keep things like integrity, generosity, gratitude, gentleness, respect, diligence, and love. Rid yourself of things like laziness, rage, envy, racism, spite, faultfinding, and vulgarity.

In the process of doing this attribute analysis, you may think that you are turning your back on your father, dishonoring him. In truth, he has always wanted you to achieve more, love more, and make fewer mistakes than he did. The best way to honor him—which is the fifth commandment, by the way—is to live your life at the highest level of excellence and connection to your Creator. Isn't that what you want for all your children?

TAKEAWAY

Look at your family history, learn from it, take the best, and chuck the rest. The past, present, and future come together at this unique point in time. Don't miss it. Your heritage has been defined by others. It has limits and liabilities. But your legacy remains undefined. It has no limits. It only has potential.

> *"If there is anything that we wish to change in our children, we should first examine it and see whether or not it is something that could better be changed in ourselves."*
> —CARL JUNG (1875–1961)

A Son Needs His Dad...

To Not Be the Jerk in the Stands

'm a good husband and a good dad.

Except at my kids' games and matches. I confess. I am the jerk in the stands.[3]

Even as I type this, you need to know that I'm not at all making light of it. I'm not shrugging it off as just an eccentricity. I am not excusing my behavior. Regretfully, I am not claiming total victory over it. True, I am actually better than I was years ago, but still I stomp around sidelines, mutter under my breath, yell at umpires and referees, and embarrass my wife and kids.

That's the worst part. I've spent thousands of hours in bleachers, lawn chairs, and leaning against fences. And I can't bear to think how many of those hours members of my own family have been regretting that I was there. How stupid am I?

In my head I can replay images of the way I have acted, and it's more than a little frustrating. It's almost like an out-of-body experience. I ask myself, *Who is this guy? Why is he making such a fool of himself?*

To be clear, I don't yell negative words at my kids or any of the young athletes. It's mostly at refs. Sometimes at the situation. Often my comments are just over-the-top, loud game analysis. Frustration boiling over. Many times I'm aggressively voicing what many of the other fans are thinking.

I will never forget my outbursts during one of Alec's baseball games in Lombard and one of Randy's wrestling matches in Sycamore. Those both took place more than a decade ago, and I still cringe when I drive past that baseball diamond and that high-school gym.

Actually the lowest point came when Max told me that if I didn't stop, he didn't want me to come to any more baseball games. That was a turning point for me. Until that moment, I wasn't sure that my sons even heard my comments from the bleachers. Let me assure you, Dad, they did. And so do your sons.

And that's why I feel the need to confess this sin in this chapter of this book. I know I'm not alone with this problem. If you can relate, allow me to suggest a few strategies for eliminating or minimizing your jerk-in-the-stands behavior.

Give your wife permission to say something. If she already does, then good for her. If you get angry when she shushes you, then you need to cut that out right away. She's trying to keep you from embarrassing yourself and the family, and prevent you from doing irreparable damage to your relationship with your son.

Walk down to the end zone or foul pole. Distance sometimes helps. Often it's the reaction of the other fans that seems to stir any disruptive enthusiasm. Getting away from the crowd reduces the zeal and reduces the decibels of your own cheers or jeers.

If you need additional help toning it down, give yourself a distraction. Hold your car keys in your hand to remind yourself to think twice before any outburst. Sharply dig them into your palm if you need to. I've used that strategy at middle-school basketball games. I've also distracted myself with game-day responsibilities like videotaping, working chain gang or concession stand, and even doing the umping myself.

Some strategies work better than others. Like I said, I'm better than I used to be.

So when it comes to my relationship with my children, that's my one fatal flaw. I have plenty of other shortcomings, but being a jerk in the stands is the one I regret most. What's yours? It may have nothing to do with being loud or boorish. It may be your habit of laying on guilt or setting unattainable expectations. It may be that you break promises or never can admit when you're wrong. It may be that you belittle their efforts or expect them to be your clone rather than follow their own dreams.

A quick review of the seven deadly sins may reveal that you are over the top when it comes to greed, sloth, envy, wrath, pride, lust, or gluttony. Some version of any of those weaknesses can get in the way of being the dad your son needs—the dad God has called you to be. Early and often, ask the One who created you for help. He's available to hear your needs and guide you toward better options 24/7/365. No matter what kind of jerk you are.

It's difficult to admit when we're wrong. It's even more difficult to admit that we can't admit that we're wrong.

> *"Get rid of all bitterness, rage, anger, harsh words, and slander, as well as all types of evil behavior. Instead, be kind to each other, tenderhearted, forgiving one another, just as God through Christ has forgiven you."*
> —EPHESIANS 4:31-32 NLT

A Son Needs His Dad...

To Insist He Come to a Men's Event

Way back in 1996, I took my two oldest sons to Soldier Field in Chicago for a Promise Keepers event. The three of us were among a stadium of guys sharing biblical truth, holding each other accountable, and learning to be better husbands, fathers, and men of God.

Alec and Randall were 16 and 13 at the time. It was the right age and the right event. A few years younger and they would have been bored. A few years older and they would have been too busy. It was one of those mountaintop experiences that fathers and sons need to do once in a while. Sure, you climb down and life goes on. But somehow your valleys are never quite as low again.

You know your son. And you can already guess how he will respond to your invitation. All I can say is once you target an event, be careful with the way you toss out the offer.

"I heard about an event at the Coliseum just for guys and it sounded like something we should do" will perk up his ears.

"A busload of men and boys from church is going to a big conference with Bible teaching and hymns and it sounded like a chance for us to bond" will most likely have him diving for his phone to make other plans for that weekend.

Of course, you don't want to trick him into coming. But if necessary you may want to play that fathering card that lays on a little guilt and should be used ever so rarely. In a quiet tone say something like, "Son, this is really important to me."

If it's a well-run event, once he's there he should be fine. Groups like Promise Keepers, Iron Sharpens Iron, and Man in the Mirror typically do a nice job of keeping it moving and presenting solid, high-energy speakers. Having been part of more than a dozen of such events as a participant and as a speaker,

I confirm that men meeting with men can be a powerful tool for strengthening families, communities, and the church. The worship proves that point.

Have you ever experienced worship surrounded only by other baritone voices booming off the walls with no annoying chirpy sopranos to distract you? It's more powerful than any scene from *Gladiator* or *300*.

When a stadium of guys sings "Our God Is an Awesome God," you can't help but believe it. That day with my sons, I am sure the cars driving by on Lake Shore Drive felt the power of our raised voices. When we sang "Lord, I Lift Your Name on High," his name was indeed lifted higher than any of the buildings in the backdrop of the Chicago skyline.

It's undeniably emotional. But don't get me wrong, the worship I'm talking about is not a superficial moment driven by volume and group dynamics. Your son would see through that in an instant. This has life-changing potential. Before the event, you need to prepare your own heart. Your checklist should include knowing who you are and knowing who God is. On a personal level, you need to be ready to simultaneously experience surrender and empowerment.

Said another way, don't drag your son to a men's event just for him. Go for yourself and your own relationship with the Creator of the universe. When your son sees God reflected in your life, that will have a greater impact than any testimony from a stranger.

TAKEAWAY

Fathers who attend a PK or ISI event with their sons receive a double blessing. They get to experience God's presence in a new way and also see him working in the lives of the young men in the same row with the same last name.

"Iron sharpens iron, so one man sharpens another."
—PROVERBS 27:17 NASB

A Son Needs His Dad...

To Work

The last time I punched a clock or headed off to work for a conventional 40- to 50-hour workweek was when my eldest, Alec, was nine years old. In the last two decades, my career path—weaving in and out from advertising to radio producer to author—has compelled me to work long, unpredictable hours. Some traveling. Late nights at the keyboard. Overnight sessions with engineers in recording studios. Weekend speaking engagements. As a result, my family never had a father who systematically left home in the morning and came home in the evening. The endearing nightly exclamation "Daddy's home!" was never chirped or cheered by my five kids.

The advantages are many. I was one of the only dads I know to volunteer in my kids' elementary school classrooms. At back-to-school night, when the sign-up sheet went around for "room moms" to help with field trips and Valentine's Day parties, I signed up. It was a blast and the teachers were always amused. During middle school, sporting events begin right after school, which means most 9-to-5 dads are missing the action. When deadlines forced me to work overtime, I didn't necessarily miss dinner with my family. I could spend 45 minutes at the table and then head back down the hallway to my office.

But don't be too jealous. Working for myself means I never really got away from client responsibilities. Never got a real vacation. And never received a regular paycheck.

I know I'm not alone in this experience. Nontraditional working hours are not so unusual anymore. Most of you dads reading this book have gone through stages of your career that had you working nights, weekends, and longer hours based on the season. That includes careers in retail, agriculture, the trades, food service, hospitality, sports, entertainment, real estate, and as any kind of independent contractor.

As a dad without a "real job," my concern has always been that my sons would not comprehend the idea of a grown man setting an alarm, leaving for work, keeping a boss happy for a full day, and then reappearing at the front door ten hours later. I never modeled that model. Does that make me a bad dad? Would my sons stumble through life not knowing how to put their nose to the grindstone?

It turns out my sons are all out of college and productive members of society. Four different personalities. Four different career paths. All with solid work ethics. Phew.

So how does that happen? Let's list four characteristics my boys might have noticed in their old dad. Ask yourself if your son sees the same values in you.

Responsibility. I didn't "go to work." But I did pay a mortgage, furnish an office, maintain the house, and sit down for dinner with my family. I hired freelance artists, engineers, voice-over talent, photographers, and video crews. I had customers and clients who counted on me and sometimes even paid their bills on time. There may be a legitimate reason a father is continuously dependent on government aid, gets hassled by bill collectors, or can't keep a job. But that has a real impact on a young man. As Josh McDowell says, "You can con a con, you can fool a fool. But you can't kid a kid."

Communication. My family knew what I did for a living. Sort of. I would talk about clients and projects. Once in a while, I would play a radio spot or show an ad I had written. I absolutely get their permission when I mention one of my kids by name in my writing. When they were younger, my wife sometimes had to remind them that "Daddy's working." Go ahead and tell your son both the joys and challenges of your work. Inviting him into your world provides a glimpse of who you are and increases the chance that he will invite you into his world once in a while.

Respect. Your son is going to treat you based on how you are treated by others. Does your wife respect you? Your friends? Your work colleagues? Your chosen career path is not nearly as important as whether you do your job well. That means staying true to your word, providing a product or service of value, delivering more than you promise, and being client sensitive and easy to work with. A man of honor doesn't make excuses, duck responsibility, deliver shoddy merchandise, or gamble away his paycheck. A growing son knows if his dad is reliable and trustworthy.

Leisure. A man who works hard also knows how to play hard. The whole family celebrates when the factory whistle blows, when Dad takes off his necktie, or when the packed-up SUV eases down the driveway for a vacation. No matter what your work schedule, your son needs to know when you transform into "fun dad" mode, shifting your focus from work to family. That's been hard for me. I love what I do and I'm constantly absorbing ideas that apply to my career. But sometimes you just have to decide *this is family time and family time is sacred.* For several years there would be a time each week when I would finally close the door to my office and literally announce, "It's weekend." Sometimes that was Friday noon. Sometimes it was Saturday evening.

If you're a man who takes responsibility seriously, communicates well with his family, earns the respect of others, and can take time off without stressing out, then your son has a high likelihood of developing a solid work ethic of his own.

I'm not sure if there's truth in the saying, "hard work is its own reward." Because work itself is, well, work. But I do believe that "hard work *brings* rewards." In addition to income those rewards include experience, relationships, new opportunities, accomplishments, recognition, gratitude, self-esteem, independence, and a good chance your son will get a job and move out of the house before he's 30.

TAKEAWAY

Men measure their value by their paycheck. And that's unfortunate. Because I know some wonderful dads who are making ends meet— but just barely. And I've met some destructive fathers who make a ton of money but are leaving a legacy of misery and bitterness.

> *"Work is an extension of personality. It is achievement.*
> *It is one of the ways in which a person defines*
> *himself, measures his worth, and his humanity."*
> —PETER DRUCKER (1909–2005)

A Son Needs His Dad...

To Break Open the Oil Paints

To their credit, my mom and dad recognized a flicker of artistic talent in yours truly. And they came through with flying colors (no pun intended) the Christmas I was in fifth grade.

I was thrilled to unwrap the Jon Gnagy Master Art Studio Set. It came in a fake-wood-grain cardboard carrying case with a metal clasp and black plastic handle. Inside were rows of real oil paints, watercolors, pastel chalks, and sketching pencils. Instruction books, sketchpads, assorted brushes, mixing trays, erasers, and sharpeners completed the set. It was awesome. I remember it well because I studied it for hours on end. I looked at it. I imagined all I would create with it. But I never actually used it. I was afraid to.

On that Christmas, more than four decades ago, my dad cheerfully and with the best intentions said four words that unintentionally doused my creative fire. He said, "Now don't waste it." With that admonition echoing in the back of my head, I dutifully committed to protecting and preserving those precious paints and brushes until I could use them properly.

Dad could have said, "Have fun. Experiment. Go crazy. When you run out, we'll get more." Those kinds of words would have inspired me to take risks, explore my gifts, and if some technique didn't work, simply start again. Today, my work could be hanging in museums around the world or I could be a starving artist in Key West. But instead, my potential as a visual artist never left the launchpad.

Let me be clear, there's no remorse. God had other plans for me and they have worked out quite nicely, thank you. My father, having been raised in the Great Depression, was quite accurate with his words. Resources shouldn't be wasted. But what Dad didn't realize is that our most valuable resources are not stuff—paints, paper, clay, wood, film, or canvas. Our greatest resources are the personal gifts and talents God has given each one of us.

One of our most important jobs as a father is to help our sons unleash their natural gifts and talents, not hold them captive.

In general, dads do a pretty good job of encouraging and resourcing our boys. In ways large and small. We might give them a set of oil paints, erect a soccer goal in the side yard, pay for guitar lessons, or invest in basketball shoes that cost more than any pair of shoes we've ever put on our own feet. I know dads who have passed up career opportunities to spend more time with their family. You may have moved to your current community for the good schools, safe neighborhoods, and well-run park district.

Just picking up this book is proof that you're the kind of dad who wants to provide your son with everything he needs to do great and glorious things.

But after we've done all that, we need to be aware that just a few words can knock our best efforts off track. You might have the best intentions. You feel like you need to maximize resources, guide him down a proven path, challenge him to give 110 percent, or protect him from disappointment. But your son might not hear what you're trying to say.

"Don't waste those oil paints!" Please don't expect your son's first painting, video short, house design, poem, or short story to be a masterpiece. First efforts are never a waste. Scribbles and typos are often the beginning of a great adventure.

"I'm thinking that the net I built should add at least two or three goals per game." When you assign undue value to your contributions, you're taking unfair credit for his future achievements. That either dismisses all his hard work or sets him up for failure.

"Start with folk songs, that's what I did." He's not you, Dad, and times have changed. Let him work out his own path to creative brilliance.

"If you don't make the team, that's fine. No pressure." Sometimes boys need to feel a little pressure. That gives them the edge they need.

Dad, each kid is different and it's your job to know them well enough to walk that fine line between setting high expectations and letting them try new things and sometimes fail. Your involvement is really all about unconditional love which comes in the form of physical touch, open communication about hopes and dreams, allowing them to learn from failure, giving way more positive feedback than negative criticism, and really just being there. In other words, open doors for your son and let them walk through. Or not.

Thinking back, my father's words are worth remembering and should be spoken with clarity and sincerity. When it comes to your son, never hesitate to point out his God-given talents. With a smile and just enough pride and a sense of expectation in your voice, you have my permission to quote the words of my truth-telling dad, "Now don't waste it."

TAKEAWAY

How about you, Dad? Do you have any gifts or talents that have been lying dormant for years? Any untapped abilities ready to be set free? Don't waste them! Let go of any accusation, guilt, or regret. Then, with your piano, camera, laptop, softball mitt, running shoes, pen, chisel, or paintbrush, simply do what you were meant to do.

> *"I am only one, but I am one. I can't do everything, but I can do something. The something I ought to do, I can do. And by the grace of God, I will."*
>
> —EDWARD EVERETT HALE (1822–1909)

A Son Needs His Dad…

To Be Disappointed in Him

D id your father have a look that stopped you in your tracks and let you know in clear terms that he was not pleased with your behavior? My dad had that valuable tool tucked away in his fathering toolbox. He didn't use it often, but when he pulled it out, it worked.

I did not want to disappoint my dad.

If your father had that look, please take a moment right now and see if you can re-create it with your own face. If you don't know what I'm talking about, give it a try anyway. Slightly clenched jaw. Lips closed. Head tilted just a bit. Eyes sad, but not glaring or squinting. Use a mirror if you have to. Pretend like you're looking right through your son into his very soul.

To get it right, imagine your nine-year-old leaving a library book on the patio overnight during a rainstorm or finding his pet goldfish floating upside-down in the fishbowl because he forgot to feed it. Part of you wants to growl, "Young man, you need to be more responsible." But if you can deliver a solid version of "the look," the words become overkill. The boy knows he messed up—you don't need to pile on. However, you do need to let him know that you expect a little more from your namesake.

To clarify, your look should be saying "I'm disappointed." Not "I hate you." Or "You're scum." Or "I'm ashamed to have you as a son." The goal is to let him know he can do better. Not to suggest he's a lost cause.

When should you use your "I'm disappointed" look? Never use it when the failure is out of his control. For example, when the deck is stacked against him or when he has truly put forth his best effort. If your son's pinewood derby car loses to the boy whose car was made by his father who happens to be a designer for Chrysler, please don't use the look. If he gets cut from the super-elite hockey team, he needs a friend, not judgment from Dad. If he studies endlessly for the National Spelling Bee, but misspells *triskaidekapho-bia* or *pneumonoultramicroscopicsilicovolcanoconiosis*, he should be earning your congratulations for making the finals, not wincing at your disapproval.

On a more serious note, Jesus modeled the best way to show disappointment to a small group of individuals he thought he could count on. In Matthew chapter 26, he asks Peter, James, and John to stand firm with him during the most crucial night of his life. That evening he had already washed feet, broken bread, shared wine, fully explained his earthly mission, and identified the two men who would betray and deny him. Heading into the Garden of Gethsemane, he turned to his three closest friends and said, "*My soul is crushed with grief to the point of death. Stay here and keep watch with me*" *(Matthew 26:38 NLT)*. All he wanted was for these guys to stay awake for 60 minutes. They didn't do it. And Jesus let them know he was disappointed. "*Then he returned to the disciples and found them asleep. He said to Peter, 'Couldn't you watch with me even one hour?'" (verse 40 NLT)*.

He didn't bash them. But he said what needed to be said. Of course, there's a lot more to that entire scene—including unrivaled spiritual battles and the destiny of humankind being determined that weekend—but I do think there's a lesson for fathers.

In general, we want to lead and teach with positive reinforcement. Laying on guilt and making our sons feel like whale dung on a regular basis is no fun and often counterproductive. But if we have set clear expectations and clear deadlines and have caught them in the act of dropping the ball, then we have the right—and even the responsibility—to let them know. We need to be able to say, "Mike, I asked you to do this. What's going on?" Or "Derek, this is not your best effort. I need you to make it right."

Sometimes, it's not easy being a dad. You need to figure out a way to confront your children in love, firmness, and grace.

TAKEAWAY

If we have shown our sons lots of love and earned their trust, it's our job to let our kids know when they have let us down. Sure, society suggests that we shouldn't make our kids feel bad. But a few words and a well-practiced look will serve them well.

"Don't throw away your friendship with your teenager over behavior that has no great moral significance. There will be plenty of real issues that require you to stand like a rock. Save your big guns for those crucial confrontations."

—JAMES DOBSON (1936–)

A Son Needs His Dad…

To Confirm That Losing Ain't All Bad

I hate to sound like one of those Succesories motivational posters, but let me toss out a few pithy quotations and we'll decide together whether or not they are true.

"Failure is success if we learn from it."

"Success is not final, failure is not fatal: it is the courage to continue that counts."

"I didn't fail the test, I just found 100 ways to do it wrong."

"If we will be quiet and ready enough, we shall find compensation in every disappointment."

"I am not concerned that you have fallen—I am concerned that you arise."

So what do you think? Should we ever consider failure a good thing? Is second place ever a victory?

I promise never to say, "It doesn't matter whether you win or lose, we're just playing for fun." Because it's critical that when your son competes, his goal is to win. In an earlier chapter we talked about a few values and ideals that are actually more important than winning. But the question we're tackling in this chapter is whether losing is ever a good thing.

May I submit that the answer depends on how your son, his teammates, his coaches, and his dad typically respond to a tough or heartbreaking loss.

If it's all sour grapes and finger-pointing then today's loss is a frustrating experience in the course of life and nothing more. But for a good coach or mentor, a loss can be a springboard for a fresh chance at greatness. It's a time to rethink and reload. A motivation to dig deeper and work harder. An opportunity to look at every play from every angle and see where improvement can be made.

Watch what happens to the two teams after a close Little League or high-school baseball game. The teams jog out to right field and left field and everyone takes a knee. The winning team has a short meeting with lots of high fives and very little instruction. The losing coach goes quite a bit longer, points out skills that need improvement, and begins to strategize areas to work on for the next practice. You've seen it dozens of times.

But wait a second. Outfielders from both teams missed hitting the cutoff man. Batters from both dugouts missed signs, took some called third strikes, and failed to advance the runner in key situations.

If it was a close game, both teams probably made the same amount of mental and physical errors. In many cases, one unlucky bounce or one bloop single was the difference between winning and losing. The biggest difference that day is that members of the losing team learned something after the game. The winners didn't. The next day, the losing coach is going to push his team a little harder—the winning coach may not.

It's no fun to lose. But I daresay, if the losing coach is getting the job done, the next time those two teams play, the result is going to be different.

This lesson goes beyond sports, of course. As a matter of fact, Paul wrote to the Romans that we shouldn't simply endure setbacks, we should actually rejoice in them. "We can rejoice, too, when we run into problems and trials, for we know that they help us develop endurance" (Romans 5:3 NLT).

─────────────────── TAKEAWAY ───────────────────

After a disappointing performance, the last thing you want to do is throw a bunch of clichés at your kid. But the fact is that while it's fun to win, most improvement happens because next time you don't want to lose again.

> *"If at first you don't succeed, destroy
> all evidence that you tried."*
> —STEVEN WRIGHT, COMEDIAN (1955–)

A SON NEEDS HIS DAD...

To Let Him Skim the Pool, Build a Tree Fort, and Sweep the Porch

When my brother and I were eight and nine years old, we got in trouble at the local Jewel Food Store.

While mom went inside we collected shopping carts in the store parking lot. It was the coolest thing in the world. We had seen the high-school boys wearing store aprons gather carts and decided to test our abilities in that grown-up arena. We did no damage. We didn't scratch any cars. As we competed against each other, Mark and I each had a nice collection of seven or eight carts when the store manager came out and did what he had to do. He wasn't nasty about it, but he explained how we were taking a job away from the stock boys, who were paid to collect carts.

Case closed. We learned our lesson. No charges were filed. It was an innocent case of two boys trying out a new skill. We saw a job that needed doing and figured we could do it.

For the record, a few years later Mark got a job as a retail clerk/bagger/cart wrangler at a different supermarket across town. A year later, I followed suit.

Fast-forward a few decades to my backyard. Rita was throwing a celebratory pool party for a group of mostly adults who had just finished a project for the school district. It was very informal and kids were invited. Early-arriving guests included a handful of adults and one bored-looking boy around nine years old. The day was windy and quite a few leaves had blown into the pool, and that set my mental gears in motion. I decided to demonstrate the fine art of pool-skimming to this young lad. It would give him something to do and be my gift to him.

My instincts were correct. I asked if he could give me a hand and showed him the swish-and-dump method of pool skimming. Five swish-and-dumps later the young man was in heaven. He had mastered a new talent, was being productive, and was no longer bored.

That's when his mom swooped in. Much to my confusion she sternly said something like "That's not your job" or "You don't have to do that." It was aimed at her son, but clearly meant for my ears. The obedient boy handed me the pool net and I was left baffled.

Was this mom scared he would fall in? Was she offended I had enlisted her son for such menial work? Was she worried her son might do a poor job and embarrass her? Or maybe she thought he would swish-and-dump on some unsuspecting guest? I still have no clue.

Allow me to extract a lesson from these two stories of boys engaging in previously untried tasks. I believe growing boys have a desire to be productive. They have a God-given yearning to identify a chore that needs doing and tackle that chore with excellence. As you consider your own young male couch potato playing hours of nonproductive video games or surrounded by three weeks of dirty laundry, that might sound slightly off base. But hear me out.

Boys build things. Model airplanes, go-carts, Tinkertoy robots, and rec-room forts made from sofa cushions, blankets, and laundry baskets. Boys do things. Race bikes, climb trees, jump off roofs, and dig holes for no reason at all. Boys love the feeling of accomplishment. Climbing to the top of junkyard heaps, shooting down rows of pop cans, and making it all the way down the toboggan slide standing up. When you read about an Eagle Scout project in the newspaper, you can't help but be a little proud of a young man who tackles a real-life project with value to the community and follows it through to completion.

A boy—like your son—is initially excited about doing work and achieving something. Especially tackling a new task and seeing how he measures up. But his enthusiasm can be crushed when someone says, "You don't have to do that." Or worse, "Stop doing that because you're doing it wrong."

So got a job to do around the house? Give it to your son. Supply him with clear goals and the right tools, then get out of his way. You may have to nudge him to get him started, but give him enough time and space. If you check in with him, don't be surprised if he's doing it slightly differently than the way you suggested. Let him try it his way. Don't micromanage. When he says the job is complete, don't find fault. Don't compare his work to that done by a professional or his older brother. As much as possible, say things like "Nicely done."

Later, when he heads off into the real world armed with a solid work ethic and a desire to do great things, he'll have you to thank.

=========== TAKEAWAY ===========

Think back to the very first buck you earned (not from your parents). Shoveling snow, delivering newspapers, bussing tables, detasseling corn, mowing lawns, whatever. Felt good, didn't it? Why would you deprive your young son of that same feeling?

"There is joy in work. There is no happiness except in the realization that we have accomplished something."

—Henry Ford (1863–1947)

A Son Needs His Dad...

To Open a Dozen Doors
to Spiritual Truth

Your son is counting on you for his worldview. There are questions he will have.

Why are we here? Does God exist? What is truth? Is there truth? Are lying, stealing, murder, and coveting wrong? Who says those things are wrong? How do you judge the character of another person? Is it even proper to judge someone else's character? How should we relate to others? How should we relate to animals, plants, and our planet? Why can't I just do what I want, when I want?

Even if your son never asks you these specific questions, you still need to provide the answers. His ability to make right choices and have any peace of mind depends on his ability to know and follow God's plan. The Bible paints a disturbing picture of people who walk in ignorance. *"They don't know where to find peace or what it means to be just and good. They have mapped out crooked roads, and no one who follows them knows a moment's peace" (Isaiah 59:8 NLT).*

This chapter will not supply answers to any of the above questions. Instead, it provides something even better. Below are 12 portals through which you can deliver spiritual truths to that boy you love so much. Some are your direct responsibility, but most of them are resources you can access with very little effort on your part. Open these 12 floodgates of truth and Satan won't stand a chance when he comes after your son.

Bedtime prayers. This is a no-brainer, Dad. Take full advantage of the last minutes of the day. Do this like it's your job. (Oh yeah, it is!) Dim the lights. Settle their hearts and minds. Untangle any confusion and frustrations of the day. Pray words that instill optimism for the morning to come. I suggest you don't say, "If I should die before I wake..." I understand the theology and sincerity of such a prayer, but why fill a young child's head with that image? Instead, speak words of praise and gratitude for all God is, all he's done, and all he will do in your son's life.

Scripture. Make sure Bibles are dusted off and opened frequently around the house. Make sure he sees you reading your Bible. Buy him a kids' devotional. As he gets older, there are masculine-themed teen study Bibles that are worth the investment. He has to make his own choice to read them, but making them available is the first step.

Church programs. If your church isn't kid-friendly, find another church. Take full advantage of trained professionals who know how to get kids excited about God. Make sure you check out what is being taught. Maybe even volunteer yourself as a teacher or AWANA leader. And don't forget to dialogue with your son about what was covered this week.

Youth group. Because of the frequent turnover of staff, most church youth groups seem to be in transition. So be patient. Schedule a meeting with you, your son, and the youth pastor and let the two of them do most of the talking. Don't ask your son if he wants to go. Just assume he'll be attending each week whether that's Sunday evening, Wednesday night, or whenever. It may be helpful to carpool and have your son invite his chums.

Mission trips and youth camp. This is an absolute must for teenage males. A well-run week or two away from home will challenge your son to leave his comfort zone, and he'll very likely make friends and memories that will last forever. He may not express any interest, but make him go. Work around his sports and summer schedules. Done right, that adventure may change his life. Really.

Bookstores. Identify a good Christian bookstore, and make it a habit to stop in when you're in the area. You browse. He browses. If he finds something— a CD, book, or even a poster or T-shirt—make the investment.

Christian radio. Not every time you get in the car, but sometimes be tuned in to the local station that broadcasts author interviews, teaching programs, and catchy praise songs. I recommend K-LOVE, American Family Radio, any

Moody Radio affiliate, and Salem Broadcasting. If your son is riding shotgun and wants to change stations, don't take it as a rejection of all things spiritual. But you should sometimes say, "No, I'm listening to this."

Dinner prayer. Pray before every meal, no matter where you are. My family holds hands around the table and I usually have a few words to say. Occasionally, I'll ask someone else to lead. Make your prayer short enough that the food doesn't get cold. In public, make it quiet, short, and sweet. It's not for show, it's to acknowledge the provider.

Teachable moments. This falls in the category of moments that you don't plan, but you need to be ready for. You've got about 173 truths you want to teach your son. Some are easy and obvious lessons such as "Don't litter" and "Wear a bike helmet." Some are more complex, such as "Life is precious" and "Keep the marriage bed pure." Spend enough time with your son, and eventually every topic you want to cover will come up in the natural ebb and flow of life.

Adventures in Odyssey. This series of half-hour radio broadcasts from Focus on the Family deserves its own bullet point. All five of my kids fell asleep to "Odysseys" into their teen years and beyond. As an old radio guy, I can't say enough about how well-written and well-produced they are. Introduce a five-year-old to the gang at "Whit's End" and he'll be hooked. In a good way.

Friends. You can't pick your son's friends. But you can choose a good neighborhood and good schools and guide him in the activities he chooses. But don't panic if his hobby is skateboarding or motocross. There are great families and not-so-great families in every school and every sport and every pastime.

His mom. Talk frequently with your son's mom about his spiritual development and moral convictions. Not to cause panic when some minor challenges pop up in his life. But to make sure you are both on the same page in choosing priorities and exposing him to positive influences.

No one is letting you off the hook, but it's good to know that you're not alone in the spiritual development of your son. Of course, his list of questions is still there and always will be. The greatest minds in history have been debating theological truths for generations. As your son gets older, I recommend you partner with him in a mutual quest for answers.

TAKEAWAY

If your son sees truth down one hallway, he may or may not walk that way. If he sees truth in every room, he'll feel at home.

"Aim at heaven and you will get earth thrown
in. Aim at earth and you get neither."
—C.S. Lewis (1898–1963)

A Son Needs His Dad...

To Teach Him How to Build a Fire. Without Matches.

have several guys in my life that are a half-generation younger than me. My kids are grown and having babies of their own. But these guys are right in the middle of being crazy, busy dads doing all the crazy, busy dad stuff. When I talk with them, I get a little envious. I miss those days.

I'm thinking specifically of Ron, who's about 15 years behind me. He's a hard-working, competitive dad with a delightful bride and four great kids. During the decade we spent in the same men's small group, it became clear that Ron was committed to being intentional about fatherhood. When his kids were toddlers, mine were in high school, which apparently made me an expert. His never-ending curiosity and questions led me to give him an early outline of my first book for fathers, *52 Things Kids Need from a Dad*. Ron's enthusiasm was one of the factors that prompted me to finish the complete manuscript.

Today, Ron still reads books for dads, pursues creative activities with his kids, and jumps online once in a while to get fresh fathering ideas. During our occasional lunch get-togethers with a couple other dads, I can always count on two things from him. First, he'll remember something I said or wrote years ago and quote it back to me. Second, he'll tell me about some wild or creative thing he's done recently with his sons that never even occurred to me back when my boys were the ages of his boys.

Which brings me to the point of this chapter. Ron happened to see a kit online for starting a campfire without matches. Sounds fun, right? Just about every dad reading this book has thought about performing that amazing feat at one time or another. But here's the difference. Ron actually ordered the kit. And used it!

How many times have you seen or heard about something and thought to yourself, "I should do this with my son"? It could be anything: A car show to drool over together. A zip line to zip down together. A trivia book to stretch your minds. A new gadget to goof with. A rocket to launch. A magic trick to baffle. A batting cage to take some cuts. A book to read together. Or any adventure to share. But 99 percent of the time we fail to follow through.

For Ron, it was an easy decision to order the relatively inexpensive kit that would provide everything you need to literally rub two sticks together to make fire. Then, even more important, he didn't wait for just the right moment. He opened it and gathered his sons and gave it a try.

This particular kit used the bow-and-drill method of spinning a wood dowel to create friction, resulting in enough heat to ignite some fibrous tinder that was also provided. Other kits came with flint and steel, a ferrocerium rod and knife blade, a magnifying glass, or some kind of parabolic mirror to focus the sun's rays. All very cool.

As he described the experience, Ron began reliving the entire fire-making event right there at the coffeehouse table. He sawed an invisible bow back and forth, blew gently on the tinder, and delighted in the small burst of imaginary flame. The other dads at the table knew any marshmallows toasted in that self-made campfire would taste better than any other marshmallows ever toasted. Yes, we were envious.

So Dad, if Ron's story has captured your imagination, make this happen. On your next wilderness adventure or right in your backyard. Do a web search for "starting a fire without matches" or "bow-and-drill fire starting." Order a kit or design your own. While you're at it, take this opportunity to teach your boys about fire safety and respecting nature.

I never started a campfire without matches together with my sons. I missed out. And so did they. Maybe I'll give it a try with my future grandsons. (You know what, I take it back. I *will* do it with that next generation of Payleitners. That's a promise.)

TAKEAWAY

When something occurs to you that would be a blast to do with your boy, take full advantage. Make that memory. Then tell some other dads about it. And then drop me an e-mail so I can pass it on to even more dads. We're all in this together.

"Look what I have created! I have made fire!"
—CHUCK NOLAND, *the character played by Tom Hanks in the film* Cast Away

A Son Needs His Dad...

To Let Boys Be Boys

This chapter is not about shaking your head and rolling your eyes when your son does something naughty—like breaking the neighbor's window with a slingshot or exploding a pop can with a firecracker. That is the 1950s version of "boys will be boys."

What needs to be said loud and clear is that boys are being exposed too early to stuff that steals their childhood. Just like girls are wearing makeup and provocative clothing too soon, boys are also being forced to grow up way before they're ready.

Instead of playing pickup games of baseball and touch football in the streets, boys with a little athletic talent are forced into programs with rosters, referees, and aggressive dads pushing them too early to achieve too much. Short seasons of organized sports are awesome and I am on record endorsing traveling sports. But we need to leave room for random, raucous play where the boys choose teams and make up their own rules.

Following the same idea, boys today spend way too much time indoors and not enough time exploring the woods, creeks, and prairies of this great land. Boys need to catch garter snakes, build tree forts, and splash into swimming holes. They need to walk on railroad tracks, sleep under the stars, and ride their bikes across town. However, moms and dads are afraid to give them that freedom. As a result, we're raising a generation of wimps who are also afraid.

But the most disturbing way that we're not letting boys be boys is that they are being exposed to pornography and sexual images at a very early age. I apologize for stirring these memories, but just about all the dads reading this chapter can recall the emotional impact of seeing images of naked women for the first time. Probably it was a magazine owned by an older brother of a friend. By today's standards it was pretty tame.

In her well-researched book *Boys Should Be Boys*, Meg Meeker, MD, suggests that what you saw and when you saw it is quite different than the graphic video images your son has been or will be exposed to. Dr. Meeker writes,

> Women in *Playboy* magazines twenty or thirty years ago were alone. While they stared seductively at the viewer, they were not engaged in a sexual act. But *Playboy* over the last few decades has been nudged aside by more graphic magazines and other media. In 1985, 92 percent of males had a *Playboy* magazine by age fifteen. Today the average age of a boy's first exposure to pornography is eleven, and where he might once have seen only a naked woman, now he is much more likely to view sex acts between partners. Nearly half of boys between the third and the eighth grade have visited Internet sites with "adult content." The more graphic the content, the more severe the trauma it inflicts on our boys.[4]

Pornography pulls families apart. For grown adults, it becomes secretive, obsessive, even addictive. It triggers physical and emotional forces that divide husbands and wives. Now think for one moment about how a graphic sex scene can derail the healthy thought patterns of a fourth-grade boy—a boy who should be catching tadpoles and tossing rocks at boxcars.

So what's a dad to do? First, control what you can control. Disconnect yourself and your family from any potential avenues where porn can enter your home or office. Don't let R-rated movies into your home on DVD, download, or cable. And let your son know about that choice you're making. Your modeling is an excellent start.

When sexualized images do creep into view, use them as a teachable moment. When the swimsuit edition of *Sports Illustrated* comes to your mailbox, go ahead and carry it all the way to the outside garbage can. Tell your son, "I didn't need it in the house and I'm doing you a favor because you don't need it either." If you have the guts, you could even say something like, "Sure, the girls are pretty, but women are so much more than that. What they're selling is not love and respect. They're not even selling swimsuits—they're using sex to sell magazines and it's not right."

That kind of honesty could lead to a frank conversation about how men need to help each other out and hold each other accountable. In 1 Corinthians, Paul warns that we should not attempt to fight temptation on our own.

We may think we're standing strong, but we're teetering over the edge of the cliff. Our only real hope is to look to God for a way out.

> *If you think you are standing firm, be careful that you don't fall! No temptation has overtaken you except what is common to mankind. And God is faithful; he will not let you be tempted beyond what you can bear. But when you are tempted, he will also provide a way out so that you can endure it (1 Corinthians 10:12-13).*

So God promises a way out. For adults, that might mean finding counselors and support groups. But your son already has a built-in advocate. Someone to help him make right choices. That's you, Dad.

Honestly, you can't prevent him from seeing stuff that is graphic and shameful. When it happens you probably won't even know about it. He will be embarrassed, feel guilty, and won't want to get lectured. As with so many issues, if you can equip him ahead of time, he'll have a much better chance of making the right decision.

The funny part is that we actually do want our sons to be curious about sex and pursue a courtship and marriage with a beautiful young lady in the not-too-distant future. A few well-chosen words or a series of long father–son conversations (not lectures) will help him achieve that kind of healthy relationship down the road.

Which brings us to one more absolute course of action. Men, kiss your wife in the kitchen. Your son needs to see that a great marriage has real passion. You know you're doing it right if your third-grader says, "Eww" or your teenager says, "Get a room."

TAKEAWAY

Once in a while, join your son on his boyhood adventures. Camping. Creek jumping. Firefly catching. Marshmallow roasting. That will make it a little easier to enter his world and initiate a nonaccusatory conversation when he starts thinking about girls and all that kind of stuff.

> *"When you're safe at home you wish you were having an adventure; when you're having an adventure you wish you were safe at home."*
>
> —Thornton Wilder (1897–1975)

A SON NEEDS HIS DAD...

To Help Him See His Truest Value

If you also have a daughter or two, you already know that boys are different than girls. Boys explore. Girls relate. Boys are more physical. Girls are more verbal. Boys play with trucks and guns. Girls really do play with dolls. Boys build forts. Girls hold tea parties.

While I was researching my book *52 Things Daughters Need from Their Dads*, it became very clear that one of the biggest differences between boys and girls is how they perceive themselves. (I hesitate to use the word *self-esteem* because so many strategies for building self-esteem are based on giving false praise for minimal effort and minimizing the need for personal responsibility.)

Anyway. Here's one of the hugest differences that you need to understand no matter how many kids you have. Just about every girl is going to pass through an extended phase in which she feels worthless. Starting about age eight, girls become assaulted with visual images of women that are impossible to live up to. When most girls (and probably your wife, as well) look in the mirror, they don't like what they see.

Boys have almost the exact opposite problem. Each boy is different, but his self-image often comes across as being invincible, egocentric, perfectly comfortable with the status quo, or put on this earth to be served, not to serve. Of course, the opposite is true. Boys are not indestructible or the center of the universe. There's always room for improvement. And a young man's father, mother, or future wife should not be expected to wait on him hand and foot.

Amazingly, the self-image problems of boys and girls are solved the exact same way. They need to look in the mirror and see that—as individuals—they are worth Jesus.

A quick theology lesson may be appropriate here.

To describe what Jesus did on the cross, theologians use the term *substitutionary atonement.* That's a fancy way of saying that we've all sinned, each of us must be punished for those sins, but Jesus paid that price for each of us when he died on the cross.

Three passages from the Bible make it clear.

> *Surely he took up our pain and bore our suffering, yet we considered him punished by God, stricken by him, and afflicted. But he was pierced for our transgressions, he was crushed for our iniquities; the punishment that brought us peace was on him, and by his wounds we are healed. We all, like sheep, have gone astray, each of us has turned to our own way; and the LORD has laid on him the iniquity of us all (Isaiah 53:4-6).*

> *God made him who had no sin to be sin for us, so that in him we might become the righteousness of God (2 Corinthians 5:21).*

> *"He himself bore our sins" in his body on the cross, so that we might die to sins and live for righteousness; "by his wounds you have been healed" (1 Peter 2:24).*

Do you get it? Jesus loved us so much that he took our place. One of my favorite terms for this act is "the Great Exchange." That paints an accurate picture of my inferior self being replaced by a new righteousness. The "old me" was nailed up on that cross and exchanged for a "new person."

All our children need to know this. And perhaps your most important job as their father is to establish an environment in which they each understand and accept that free gift of grace. But daughters and sons will be impacted by such a revelation in different ways.

Boys and girls both receive eternal life, the indwelling of the Holy Spirit, and an inheritance in the kingdom of God. But a girl should now be able to look in the mirror and see the resurrected Jesus. Beautiful and worthy. And a boy needs to look in the mirror and see reflected back at him Jesus as the Servant King. A leader who finds his purpose in giving of himself to others.

When your son's peers are acting macho or being slackers, your son will be able to say—or think—*What would Jesus do?* If he has been living with God's grace for more than a few years, there's a good chance he may slide through that cocky, strong-willed period of his life with a little more humility and respect for authority. Over those early years, you can help by intentionally and sincerely pointing out how God has been working in his life. Anticipate moments when he shows compassion to a friend, patience with a sibling, or generosity with a stranger.

Let him know when you see God's love reflected in his words and actions. This isn't false praise or artificial self-esteem-building, which ultimately falls flat. As a new creation, your son will literally have new gifts and points of view that he may not even realize.

Think about the response from the Lord's servants when he thanks and blesses them for feeding, visiting, clothing, and caring for him. They were confused. They said, *"Lord, when did we see you hungry and feed you, or thirsty and give you something to drink? When did we see you a stranger and invite you in, or needing clothes and clothe you? When did we see you sick or in prison and go to visit you?" (Matthew 25:37-39).* They don't know the magnitude of their good deeds. They don't fully realize their selfish hearts have been exchanged for servants' hearts.

Dad, you are the best person to witness and point out how Christ has transformed your son's life. You know the before and after. You are in a unique position to help him see how valuable he is. Make sure he experiences, celebrates, and cherishes the Great Exchange.

TAKEAWAY

In this case, what's good for your son is good for every member of your family. Including you, Dad.

"Do not think of yourself more highly than you ought, but rather think of yourself with sober judgment, in accordance with the faith God has distributed to each of you."

—Romans 12:3

A Son Needs His Dad...

To Schedule Mountaintop Connections

A recurring theme of this book is that day-to-day connection points matter most. Ignoring your son 362 days a year and then spending a long weekend doing something fabulous is not effective fathering.

But that doesn't mean we shouldn't pursue father–son getaways and events that take planning and a significant investment of time and money. There's no denying that big-event experiences have a certain value. Memories almost certainly will be made. But sometimes the stars align and they create new, almost magical bonds that you and your son will remember forever.

I asked a few dads to share their mountaintop moments.

In 2008, Dan took his young-adult son David to a Packers game. Nothing really amazing there, except it happened to be the playoff game that became known as the "Snow Bowl" when some 17 inches of snow fell on Green Bay. More than 36,000 fans didn't show up, but this father and son drove four hours north to see Brett Favre's last victory at Lambeau Field. Dan recalls his shivering son turning to him during the game and saying, "This is perfect." Dan was worried about the four-hour drive home, but as soon as they left the city of Green Bay, the snow disappeared.

In 2011, Dave and his 15-year-old son, Sam, lived the dream of backpacking the mountainous trails of Philmont Scout Ranch. Their crew of nine Boy Scouts and three leaders each carried a backpack with all the provisions they would need to endure the 11-day trek up and down Mt. Baldy. Three days into the trip, fatigue, altitude, and an overstuffed backpack caught up with Sam. Dave didn't judge or say, "Suck it up." Instead, they sat down and strategized about what items they could leave behind, moved a couple items to Dad's pack, and Dave explained the common phenomenon of the "third-day factor" suffered by many expeditions. "Once you get past that hurdle," he told his son, "the body begins to compensate with a new supply of energy for the fourth day and beyond." Of course, there is no "third-day factor," and perhaps Sam even knew his dad was making the whole thing up. But it worked, and the entire crew made it to the summit. On the way down the mountain, Sam heroically moved items from his 48-year-old dad's backpack to his.

With his wife's blessing, Dick would plan canoe trips down the Wisconsin River and ski trips to the Rockies with their three boys. He scheduled months in advance and prepped the gear meticulously. Kevin, Tim, and Charlie each knew that when they turned eight years old, they could finally join Dad on the next adventure. Last year, Dick didn't plan the long weekend ski trip to Utah. He didn't have to. His sons—now in their thirties and forties—made it happen. At 62, Dick didn't miss having to worry about the travel details. And he also didn't miss a single downhill run.

Jim was looking forward to spending quality time with his 23-year-old son, Andrew, during a 10-day mission trip to the Amazon. Unfortunately, the mission agency hired a girl that Andrew had dated back in high school to travel along as photographer. The unwelcome distraction took an unexpected turn and—right there in the Amazon rain forest—Jim got the privilege of witnessing his son falling in love with his future bride.

Take your son to an NFL game, scout expedition, ski trip, or mission trip and it may turn out...swell. Or God may orchestrate the circumstances to be a once-in-a-lifetime father–son experience that changes you both forever. Dan, Dave, Dick, and Jim, I salute you for going the extra mile...and congratulations for raising fine sons.

But make note, Dad. You don't always have to leave the state to have a mountaintop experience with your son. Dennis asked his son Quinn's high-school basketball coach if he could start a voluntary Bible study with some of the players and fathers. The coach agreed, but Quinn wasn't sure his teammates would go for it. How did it turn out? During the next two seasons more than a dozen fathers and sons met once a week to study God's Word and talk about life. Dennis and Quinn—and all those men—will tell you those hours together raised their relationship to a new altitude that remains to this day.

════════════════ TAKEAWAY ════════════════

Dad, schedule a time to intentionally get out of your comfort zone with your son. That will reveal who he is and who you are.

"It is not the mountain we conquer but ourselves."
—Sir Edmund Hillary (1919–2008)

A Son Needs His Dad...

To Say Yes, So You Can Say No

For boys, I believe in TV watching, video-game playing, loud music listening, and lots of other things that some parents say are bad for kids. I also believe in staying up past midnight and eating as much ice cream as fast as possible.

Allow me to clarify. Having a couple favorite TV shows you watch as a family is not a bad thing. If you look hard enough, there is some well-produced programming. You might be able to share a few laughs watching sitcoms that aren't too raunchy. If the characters start making bad decisions, you can always use it as a teachable moment.

If your son masters one—not all—of the latest video games, he'll feel like he's in the loop and keeping up with his peers, which is important for boys over eight years old.

Taking your son to a rock concert where the subwoofers shake your inner organs and your ears ring the entire ride home is a memory the two of you will share forever. Make it a rare, special event.

Sometimes you and your son have to stay up past midnight to catch a lunar eclipse, the aurora borealis, or game seven of the World Series. Mom might be reluctant, but a dad knows that some things are more important than sleep.

And of course, if there's an ice-cream-eating contest, sign him up. And sign yourself up as well.

There's a beauty and boldness in these moments of permission and excess. Breaking the routine with your boy prepares him for the unexpected twists and turns of life. But please make sure to acknowledge that these choices are indulgences. As with so many things, a little bit of television, video games, concerts, ice cream, and late-night adventures goes a long way. Less is more.

Saying "Yes" whenever reasonable is a great parenting strategy. It feels good to spoil your kids once in a while. But the best part about saying "Yes" is that it gives you the conviction to say "No."

Making decisions as a dad is tough enough. You don't have to explain every decision you make to a six-year-old. Occasionally, you may want to explain your reasoning. "We're taking this road to the park to avoid construction." "We're putting olives on the pizza because I like olives." "We're only reading one book tonight because I have something important to do with mom." Then, if he responds with some kind of whining or debate, perhaps you skip the park that day, serve him PB&J instead of pizza, or read zero books tonight.

Like so many great parenting strategies, we don't have to make this up. It's straight out of God's Word. In Matthew 5:37, Jesus teaches, "Let your 'Yes' be 'Yes,' and your 'No,' 'No.' For whatever is more than these is from the evil one" (NKJV). Did you get that? If you change your mind often and your word is wishy-washy, that's Satan having his way with you and your family.

Your son needs to see a man who assesses a situation, takes into account many different factors, makes the best decision possible, and then sticks with it. If it works out, Dad, go ahead and take some of the credit. If it doesn't work out, make sure you take most of the blame. No excuses.

Your son knows the family can't go to Disney World every weekend. He knows you won't buy him a candy bar every time you run into a convenience store or gas station. He knows you're not going to buy him a minibike to terrorize the neighborhood. When he asks, he's just testing you. Maybe you'll say yes. Maybe you'll say no. But he'll only ask once. Because you have firmly established that your yes means yes, and your no means no.

TAKEAWAY

For the first decade of your son's life, your word should be solid gold. Later, if your middle-schooler comes to you with some reasonable input or new information, you have the right to change your mind. But again, that's your choice.

> *"The art of leadership is saying no, not saying yes. It is very easy to say yes."*
> —TONY BLAIR (1953–)

A Son Needs His Dad...

To Give Your Blessing

A number of years back, Gary Smalley and John Trent published a book titled *The Blessing*, and not long ago Jim McBride wrote a very practical book, *Rite of Passage*.

The books—backed up with biblical examples—suggest dads be intentional about creating a moment in time or even a ceremony in which we tell our boys one at a time, *"You are my beloved son. These are your gifts. This is what matters. Here are a handful of truths to hold on to. I am so proud of you."*

To be sure, those words and feelings need to be part of everyday life. But delivering them with intentionality as your son approaches adulthood can give him a foundation upon which he can build for the rest of his life.

Orchestrating a "rite of passage" can be anything from a father–son walk in the woods to an elaborate ritual involving a host of mentors, symbolic gifts, and a keepsake guidebook for life filled with letters and quotations. It could be an hour or a weekend.

This is such a great idea that I have to ask, "Why would any father of a young teenage boy *not* do this?" What an awesome idea!

Well, I guess I'm a bad dad. Even as I type this, I am envious of any fathers who really took this idea and made it happen. I considered it. I had my chances, but I never really did anything official. I had plenty of excuses.

- I thought I had plenty of time. But then suddenly my sons were off to high-school activities and college.

- I didn't want to do a mediocre job of such a critical moment in time. So...I didn't do anything.

- I missed my opportunity with Alec, so how could I plan something for his three younger brothers?

- Didn't I already have plenty of quality father–son moments with my boys? But come on, how can you have too many connection points?

- I made the excuse that the whole idea is a little over-the-top and silly. But I was dead wrong about that. It would have been awesome. I should have done it four times, once for each of my four boys.

- I thought frequent activities with all my sons together would make up for a one-on-one moment. But doesn't each young man deserve to see himself as a unique, gifted individual?

I'm thinking back to a moment in our church lobby. More than 20 years ago. A father approached me with the idea of organizing a weekend for the two of us to take our oldest sons and do some kind of rite of passage ceremony. It was a great idea, but it was a busy season for me. I didn't pursue it and the opportunity was gone. I don't know if that other father ever followed through.

So there you have it. I am totally recommending you do something I never did.

For inspiration, take a look at a powerful passage from the fifth book of the Bible. As Israel was preparing to enter the Promised Land, Moses delivered an address that included principles for godly living. He acknowledged that every man has a choice to make and challenged each man to choose this very day.

> Look, today I am giving you the choice between a blessing and a curse! You will be blessed if you obey the commands of the LORD your God that I am giving you today. But you will be cursed if you reject the commands of the LORD your God and turn away from him and worship gods you have not known before (Deuteronomy 11:26-28 NLT).

This is your chance to guide your son to choose God's blessing for his life, not a curse. Start by doing just a little research. Grab the book by McBride or by Trent and Smalley. Then pick a weekend or just a Sunday afternoon. Force yourself to write down a short list of truths you want to pass on. It could be a few key verses from Scripture. Or maybe a funny top-ten list from you to him. It could be inspired by chapters from this book.

Maybe invite your son's best friend and his father to join you. Ask your youth pastor for resources. Other ideas include giving a gift such as a sword, medallion, cross, ring, Bible, or scrapbook. Do some solid preparation. But if you start to overthink it, you might never do it.

Unless your son is already out the door, do this. Pick a date on the calendar and give him a blessing. Your blessing. No excuses.

TAKEAWAY

Day after day, a father watches a little boy grow, but one day he will look back with awe to realize the boy has become a man.

> *"[Jacob] blessed Joseph and said, 'May the God before whom my fathers Abraham and Isaac walked faithfully, the God who has been my shepherd all my life to this day, the Angel who has delivered me from all harm— may he bless these boys. May they be called by my name and the names of my fathers Abraham and Isaac, and may they increase greatly on the earth.'"*

—Genesis 48:15-16

A Son Needs His Dad...

To Calmly Stop the Tractor

A friend of mine told me a defining moment in his relationship with his dad.

He was only about 5 or 6, but Glen remembers the entire incident. His dad was plowing that day. It was just another typical, critical day in the life of a farmer. Always watching the skies. Always running the progress of the growing season through his mind. Row after row. Acre after acre.

Glen saw his dad on the tractor and ran into the field. He was old enough to run fast, but not old enough to know the risk.

Boys go through stages like that as they grow—at age 3, 6, and 12. Physically they can do things, but their common sense hasn't kicked in yet. They don't see the danger. Later—at 16, 20, 22—they know exactly what they're doing but believe they're indestructible. They think they're immune to the danger.

That day on that family farm, Glen was never actually at risk. His father saw him coming through the rows and calmly shut down the rig. As Glen tells it, however, his mother was frantic. Even after the tractor was shut down, she ran from the house shouting her son's name.

Before she reached her husband and son, Glen recalls the exact words of his father. He knelt down and said, "I know you knew what you were doing and didn't think you were in any danger. But, son, you're in trouble. It's your Mom's job to take care of you and you scared her. I'll help you out, though."

And sure enough, Glen's mom reached the scene and let her son know that he had done something very wrong. She was scared to death for him. He could have gotten hurt. What if Dad hadn't seen him? She said everything a frantic mom would say in that scenario. And Glen and his father didn't disagree.

They both understood how mom had to express anger and relief, and even toss on some guilt and a "shame on you."

Glen's dad gave him a great gift that day. An understanding of how families work. That moms and dads are different. Moms take care of their kids. Dads watch out for their kids.

Best of all—from that point on—Glen knew that he and his father were a team. He describes how that event opened the door for him to talk to his father about anything at all for his entire life.

Dad, when your son makes a mistake, take a moment to assess the situation. Make sure he's safe and no further damage is imminent. Then, if he already knows he's messed up or is about to suffer significant repercussions, let him know everything's going to be okay and he can count on you. If he admits guilt and takes full responsibility, there's no reason to pile on more.

Sure, there should be repercussions. Maybe six-year-old Glen can't leave the porch for a couple weeks. Maybe your son loses his phone or car privileges. Maybe he has to pay for the ripped screen or smashed taillight. But once he's learned his lesson and paid the penalty, case closed.

On the other hand, if he's clueless or insists he did no wrong, then step in with authority and conviction, and set him straight. Make the punishment fit the crime. Don't abandon him, but make sure justice is served.

If your young son steals a candy bar, he needs to take it back and apologize to the grocer. And maybe stand silently through a lecture about honesty. You may want to call ahead and clue the proprietor in on your goal for that meeting. If your son gets caught at a beer party and gets suspended from the football team, that's a choice he made. While all the other parents threaten the coach and hire lawyers, insist that your son faces the penalty prescribed by the student-athlete honor code.

If he drops out of college, gets arrested for smoking pot, or gets his girlfriend pregnant, it won't be pleasant, but you do want him to come to you. You're not required to rescue him, but he needs wise counsel and you've never let him down before. If he goes elsewhere, he's very likely going to get some bad advice.

No matter what, make him glad that you are on his side. He can come to you and you won't raise your voice or make threats. There may be repercussions, but Dad's involvement is going to make the situation better.

Just like Glen saw his dad calmly stop the tractor and explain the situation, see if you can do that in each and every crisis situation.

━━━━━━━━━━━━━━ TAKEAWAY ━━━━━━━━━━━━━━

Dad, face any crisis with efficient action, calm assessment, and a partnership with your son. Demonstrate he can trust you. Make him glad when he asks for your help.

> *"Farmers who wait for perfect weather never plant. If they watch every cloud, they never harvest. Just as you cannot understand the path of the wind or the mystery of a tiny baby growing in its mother's womb, so you cannot understand the activity of God, who does all things. Plant your seed in the morning and keep busy all afternoon, for you don't know if profit will come from one activity or another—or maybe both."*
>
> —ECCLESIASTES 11:4-6 NLT

A Son Needs His Dad...

To Teach Him How to Shake Hands

In the early part of your church service, are you given a chance to shake hands with the people around you? Some churches call it "the sign of peace."

How does your son do with that? It's actually a pretty good opportunity to make sure he knows how to shake hands and show respect to his elders. It's also a time when you can help a young man who might be a little shy to start to move out of his comfort zone. The time frame is limited—10 to 20 seconds—and so he really only has to grit his teeth and tolerate any uneasiness for a moment. If he turns and shakes two or three hands, that's an easy victory.

You can watch how he's doing out of the corner of your eye, but mostly you should be modeling positive handshaking and greeting those around you. Any teaching you do should come long after you've left the church building. Correcting him, chiding him, or embarrassing him in the pew is a lose-lose situation. He's not learning anything. And you're driving him even more into his shell.

Later, when it's just you and him, go ahead and walk him through the main elements of a good handshake. Eye contact. Palm vertical. Extend your arm halfway to the other person. Tell him to completely slide his hand into the other person's hand until the base of their thumbs meet. (None of that wimpy fingertip stuff.) Firm grip, but not a death squeeze. Then explain that a proper handshake consists of a single (or maybe one and half) pumps. Not too big, not too small. Let your son know that in church he can usually get by without saying anything. A smile and head nod is all it takes. Out in public, he will need to speak a word or two: "Hello" or "Hi, nice to meet you." It's also an appropriate time to exchange names.

Of course, this lesson is kind of amusing with a boy who's six or seven. He will eagerly listen to every word concerning how to act like an adult. But if he's closer to ten years old, he's going to act like he already knows everything. That's how fifth-grade boys are. They want to learn all the important stuff about being a man, but they don't want you to know that they don't know. Get it?

Beyond handshakes, there are all kinds of lessons in social etiquette your son needs. When it comes to table manners, Mom is probably more concerned than you. Napkins in laps. Elbows off the table. Bringing your food to your face, not your face to your food. Chewing with mouth closed. Using the proper fork. Rita even had a dinner-table rule that no one could have seconds until she had finished her first serving. That's a pretty good rule to minimize food wolfing.

Fathers should certainly support their wives' emphasis on all these courtesies. But you will also want to take the lead in some of the more manly social skills. Especially in group settings.

When called upon to pray before a meal, three sentences are ideal. Thanks for God's provision. Thanks for the people around the table. Blessings on the food and event. Amen.

When called upon to make a toast, if you go longer than a minute, you've lost your audience. Share one memory. One joke. One sincere appreciation. And raise your glass. If you're the best man at a wedding, you can stretch to 90 seconds. But please, please don't embarrass the groom in front of his new in-laws.

At the end of a group restaurant experience, someone has to pick up the tab. A generation ago, separate checks were torture, but today's restaurant technology decreases the hassle. So if your son is out with friends, let him know it's acceptable to ask the server and she'll usually be glad to oblige. If it's a smaller group, tell him it's the manly thing to do—once in a while—to reach for the check. But not too often, and never to show off. Over the course of a year, every guy should pull his own weight.

On tipping, you really should leave 20 percent to your server. How much is that? Just double the check and move the decimal point one numeral over to the left. The tip on a $34 tab is $6.80, rounded up to $7.00. Make sense? Do you think that's too generous? Tell your son, if he can't afford to tip properly, then he can't afford to go out.

And then there's urinal etiquette. Like at an ATM, if there's a line, give the current user plenty of room. No guy wants another guy scoping out his PIN number or his private parts. It there's a row of urinals with plenty of room, instruct your son to choose the farthest location. You may want to teach him to flush with his elbow. And, for heaven's sake, to wash and dry his hands.

There are quite a few examples of social etiquette your son needs to learn from you but you cannot insist upon. For instance, you might tell him it's considered impolite to wear a hat indoors, answer his cell phone in public, or text at the dinner table. He might say that's all perfectly acceptable behavior. And in his social circles he might be right. Still insist there's no excuse for blowing his nose in public, overloading his plate at the buffet line, or being rude to hotel servers, hostesses, cashiers, hotel clerks, and others.

Dad, you should be modeling all this stuff, even if you're not very good at it. When in doubt, ask your wife. Or check out ArtOfManliness.com. It's a pretty clean website filled with stuff you can share and laugh about with your son.

═══════════════════ **TAKEAWAY** ═══════════════════

Teach your son how to shake hands, make a toast, talk to a maître d', hail a cab, and leave a tip before he has to know those things. It's much more difficult to teach him afterward, because then he has to admit he didn't do it right the first time.

"Etiquette means behaving yourself a little
better than is absolutely essential."
—WILL CUPPY (1884–1949)

A SON NEEDS HIS DAD...

To Never Forget He's Watching and Learning

Whether you realize it or not, you are making choices 24/7/365. And your son is watching. Are you...

- *Forgiving others? Or holding grudges?*
- *Modeling delayed gratification? Or buying the latest and greatest version of every gadget and gizmo early and often?*
- *Tossing candy wrappers out the car window? Or leaving your campsite or picnic area cleaner than when you arrived?*
- *Cheering your team? Or jeering the other team?*
- *Being a good neighbor? Or playing your music too loud and letting your dandelions take over the neighborhood?*
- *Calmly working out the details? Or getting ticked at every minor setback?*
- *Being a good son and son-in-law? Or grousing about having to waste your vacation time with your extended family?*
- *Watching TV that turns your mind to mush? Or daring to do the amazing act of turning off (or even unplugging) the idiot box once in a while?*
- *Promoting selflessness? Or selfishness?*
- *Demonstrating a work ethic? Or expecting others to provide?*
- *Picking up your dirty socks and leaving the toilet seat down? Or the opposite?*

- *Choosing courage? Or the easy way out?*
- *Having convictions? Or letting the situation determine what's right or wrong?*
- *Standing up for your convictions? Or having no depth of character?*
- *Acknowledging God as the Creator of the universe? Or dismissing you, your son, your family, and the universe as an accident?*
- *Choosing faithfulness to your wife? Or lusting for and flirting with other women?*
- *Giving him a vision of eternity? Or suggesting that you might as well party hard because life on this planet is all you get?*
- *Working toward racial reconciliation? Or perpetuating stereotypes?*
- *Opening God's Word for answers? Or thinking you know everything you will ever need to know?*
- *Staying fit? Or channel-surfing and couch-potatoing?*
- *Eating one less slice of pizza than you really need? Or eating one more slice of pizza than you really need?*
- *Wearing your seat belt? Or not caring about your loved ones?*
- *Catching your favorite NFL or college team on TV? Or watching every down of every game all weekend long?*

No one's perfect. Mistakes will be made. So please don't beat yourself up. Maybe look at it this way. Even when you mess up, that gives you a fresh chance to model a new and improved course of action: Admit your mistake. Ask forgiveness. Then fix what you broke or pledge to do better next time.

When you review this list—no matter how you did—it's a good idea to do a regular personal inventory on what character traits your son is seeing in you. Can you look in the mirror and say, "Keep up the good role modeling work?" Or is it more, "That's the best you can do? You're a dad, for crying out loud!"

Did this chapter leave you feeling a little beat-up? Sorry about that. Try reviewing the above list from an entirely different perspective. Ask yourself this: *What kind of character traits would I like to see in my son ten or twenty years from now?*

━━━━━━━━━━━━━━ TAKEAWAY ━━━━━━━━━━━━━━

Like father, like son.

> *"If a man watches three football games in a row, he should be declared legally dead."*
>
> —ERMA BOMBECK (1927–1996)

A Son Needs His Dad…

To Pass the Torch

The summer my dad was dying of bone and liver cancer, one of his four kids—all of us in our fifties—stopped by each night to make sure he had his meds and got tucked safely into bed. My mom was there, but it was more than she could handle. My sister Sue managed the schedule.

So, two nights a week I was scheduled to drive all the way across town to see my dad and mom. Whether I wanted to or not.

Well, you can imagine what happened during those weeks. Mary Kay, Mark, Jay, and Sue—plus our spouses and many of the grandkids—had the privilege of watching a good man approach death with dignity. We witnessed Dad's increasing loss of muscle tone, growing confusion, and frequent long pauses as he considered his next words and choices. But he never complained about the pain.

I rarely looked forward to those trips to Carriage Oaks Senior Living Center. But when I got there, I was glad. The medical part of it—insulin, morphine, pills, and so on—was incidental. Every single visit left me with a sense of awe and appreciation for the legacy my parents had given to our family.

About five years earlier, when his bladder was removed in his first battle with cancer, my dad had told me he was "ready for all of this to be over." But really he wasn't ready. And I wasn't ready to let him go. I even told him so. I said, "Dad, there's still stuff you need to do. We still need you."

It turns out, I was right. Over his last five years, he gave much love, conveyed many truths, and even welcomed four new members to his family—two granddaughters-in-law and his first two great-grandchildren. During that time, he counseled me in some important areas. Most important, I saw him grow in a new way in his relationship with Christ. It was a wonderfully worthwhile five years.

During that last summer, one of the evenings I walked in the door of their Carriage Oaks apartment, I found my parents in the bathroom. Mom was leaning against the sink. Dad was on the tile floor wedged between the bathtub and toilet. In his weakened state, he had slipped while trying to get to his walker. They weren't panicking. They weren't embarrassed. They were just trying to figure out what to do. He had not been lying there very long and they knew I was coming. My instinct was simply to pick him up, but Mom stopped me. She said, "No, you'll hurt yourself." She wanted to call the building handyman. Which, of course, was ridiculous because he was like 70 years old himself. But that's the way moms are sometimes.

I bent over and picked up my dad—who was surprisingly light—and carried him to his bed. I hung around a bit, did Dad's bedtime rituals, and then drove home.

Later, when I was talking to my brother, Mark, he said the same thing had happened to him. Dad had fallen. Mom was worried that Mark would hurt himself. But my brother effortlessly picked Dad up and got him in his chair.

Mark and I were both gratified that we had had the opportunity and the ability to literally pick Dad up when he needed us. Moving beyond the symbolism, there's great satisfaction in being part of the *circle of life*. I won't quote Mufasa, Simba, or Rafiki here or any lines from *The Lion King*. But I will say that as fathers we need to give our sons permission to grow up and become stronger than we are. Eventually replacing us. Taking their rightful place as head of the family.

The rest of this chapter is a message to my four sons.

I hope I die with dignity. I hope you're around those final weeks. I hope I don't cause you too much despair. (I also hope it's at least two or three decades from now.) I hope you feel comfortable picking me up when I fall. Mostly, I hope that I've earned the right to expect you would do that for me. Make sense?

TAKEAWAY

The day when a father needs his son more than the son needs his father should not come as a surprise.

> *"Every father should remember that one day his son*
> *will follow his example instead of his advice."*
> —Charles F. Kettering (1876–1958)

A Son Needs His Dad...

To Be There

D riving home from the University of Illinois at Champaign-Urbana as midnight approached, I couldn't help but wonder whether our trip was worth the trip.

My wife, Rita, was asleep in the passenger seat and I was still scratching my head trying to figure out what invisible force had led us to make the three-hour trip down to campus. Six hours back and forth.

A couple of times a week we talked on the phone with our son Randy, a junior English major, and he had been telling us how much fun he was having playing intramural football. The diving catches, trick plays, and team camaraderie. In many ways, he said, it was more fun than high-school sports. So—in the middle of the workweek—we got in the car and went. Did I mention it was six hours back and forth?

Rita and I timed our 160-mile trek to arrive just in time for his 8 p.m. co-ed intramural flag-football game. If you know about such things, you know that's unheard of. Parents just don't go there. Not that it's frowned upon; it's just out of the ordinary. But we had been invited. We mentioned to Randy it would be fun to watch him play again and he said, "Come on down!"

It was a brisk autumn night; football was in the air. The teams began to assemble and stretch out, just like real athletes. Randy introduced us to a few of his teammates who were genuinely perplexed by our presence. An official referee checked in. The cheering section would be limited to Rita, me, and a player on crutches sidelined from an injury in a previous game. But even that got me hoping that I was about to enjoy a real football game with real plays and aggressive strategies.

Unfortunately, midterms were coming up. And the other team was two or three players short. Apparently, their less-dedicated athletes thought studying was more important than intramurals. So, as happens, the game was forfeited. Not a big deal, unless you had just driven 160 miles to stand on the sidelines.

We took Randy out for pie and coffee. Which, looking back, was more gratifying than watching any football game. After all, how often do you get a chance to stop in the middle of the week and just talk with your young-adult son? I don't remember any specific topic, but I did have the sense that Rita and I were watching our son turn into an adult right before our eyes. Then we hit the road home.

Behind the wheel, I had plenty of time to allow the lessons of the evening to come together. This journey called life has all kinds of noteworthy milestones—birthdays, graduations, end-of-the-year concerts, championship games, and award ceremonies. Any good dad—like you or me—is going to clear his calendar and attend those big events. That earns the gold star, right?

Well, yeah. But big events are not when life happens.

Life happens during the small moments. Raking leaves. Street hockey. Driveway hoops. Trips to the hardware store. Clearing debris from the storm sewer in the middle of a rainstorm. Debating over the best NFL running back. Hashing out a theological question from that morning's sermon. Flushing a dead goldfish. Burying a beloved dog in the backyard. Washing the car. Polishing shoes. Making ice cream. Digging out a tree stump. Asking your son to program your smartphone. Putting the chain back on his bike. Leaning against his bedroom doorway and comparing frustrations you're having at work and he's having at school. Teaching him to tie a tie. Sharing a box of cereal at 2 a.m. Intramural football games. Small moments that add up.

Pulling into our driveway well after midnight, I realized God had been guiding me in my fathering for the last eight hours and the last 20 years. A football game that never happened led directly to an overwhelming flood of gratitude that God had called me to be a dad. To be there. Every day. What a privilege.

TAKEAWAY

If you take the time to listen, God will give you a soul craving to be there for your son. Don't miss it.

"I believe that what we become depends on what our fathers teach us at odd moments, when they aren't trying to teach us."

—Umberto Eco (1932–)

Notes

1. Chapter adapted in part from Jay Payleitner, *52 Things Kids Need from a Dad* (Eugene, OR: Harvest House Publishers, 2010), pp. 91-92.

2. Chapter adapted from Payleitner, *52 Things Kids Need*, pp. 137-139.

3. Chapter adapted from Jay Payleitner, *52 Things Wives Need from Their Husbands* (Eugene, OR: Harvest House Publishers, 2011), pp. 85-86.

4. Patricia Greenfield in *Journal of Applied Developmental Psychology*, as quoted by Meg Meeker, *Boys Should Be Boys* (New York: Ballantine Books, 2009), pp. 65-66.

Once Upon a Tandem

The One-Year Life Verse Devotional

52 Things Kids Need from a Dad

365 Ways to Say "I Love You" to Your Kids

52 Things Wives Need from Their Husbands

One-Minute Devotions for Dads

If God Gave Your Graduation Speech

If God Wrote Your Birthday Card

52 Things Daughters Need from Their Dads

52 Things Husbands Need from Their Wives

About the Author

Jay Payleitner is a dad. But he pays his mortgage and feeds his family working as a freelance writer, ad man, motivational speaker, and radio producer with credits including *Josh McDowell Radio*, *WordPower*, *Jesus Freaks Radio*, and *Today's Father with Carey Casey*. Jay served as the Executive Director for the Illinois Fatherhood Initiative and is a featured writer/blogger for the National Center for Fathering. He is the author of the bestselling *52 Things Kids Need from a Dad*, *365 Ways to Say "I Love You" to Your Kids*, *The One-Year Life Verse Devotional*, and the acclaimed modern parable *Once Upon a Tandem*. Jay and his high-school sweetheart, Rita, have four married sons and one daughter and live in St. Charles, Illinois. You can invite Jay to speak on marriage and parenting and read his weekly dadblog at jaypayleitner.com.

fathers.com
NATIONAL CENTER FOR FATHERING

The National Center for Fathering

We believe *every* child needs a dad they can count on. At the National Center for Fathering, we inspire and equip men to be the involved fathers, stepfathers, grandfathers, and father figures their children need.

The National Center was founded by Dr. Ken Canfield in 1990 as a nonprofit scientific and education organization. Today, under the leadership of CEO Carey Casey, we continue to provide practical, research-based training and resources that reach more than one million dads annually.

We focus our work in four areas, all of which are described in detail at fathers.com:

Research. The Personal Fathering Profile, developed by a team of researchers led by Ken Canfield, and other ongoing research projects provide fresh insights for fathers and serve as benchmarks for evaluating the effectiveness of our programs and resources.

Training. Through Championship Fathering Experiences, Father-Daughter Summits, online training, small-group curricula, and train-the-trainer programs, we have equipped over 80,000 fathers and more than 1000 trainers to impact their own families and local communities.

Programs. The National Center provides leading edge, turnkey fathering programs, including WATCH D.O.G.S. (Dads Of Great Students), which involves dads in their children's education and is currently in more than 1300 schools in 36 states. Other programs include Fathering Court, which helps dads with significant child-support arrearages, and our annual Father of the Year Essay Contest.

Resources. Our website provides a wealth of resources for dads in nearly every fathering situation, many of them available free of charge. Dads who make a commitment to *Championship Fathering* receive a free weekly e-newsletter full of timely and practical tips on fathering. *Today's Father*, Carey Casey's daily radio program, airs on 600-plus stations. Listen to programs online or download podcasts at fathers.com/radio.

Make your commitment to Championship Fathering

Championship Fathering is an effort to change the culture for today's children and the children of coming generations. We're seeking to reach, teach, and unleash 6.5 million dads, creating a national movement of men who will commit to LOVE their children, COACH their children, MODEL for their children, ENCOURAGE other children, and ENLIST other dads to join the team. To make the Championship Fathering commitment, visit fathers.com/cf.

Also by Jay Payleitner

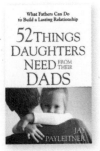

52 Things Daughters Need from Their Dads
What Fathers Can Do to Build a Lasting Relationship

The days of tea parties, stuffed doggies, and butterfly kisses are oh-so-important, but they don't last forever. So how can a dad safeguard his daughter so she grows up strong, healthy, beautiful, and confident?

Jay Payleitner has given valuable, man-friendly advice to thousands of dads in his bestselling *52 Things Kids Need from a Dad*. Now Jay guides you into what may be unexplored territory—*girl land*—and gives you ways to...

- date your daughter
- be on the lookout for "hero moments" and make lasting memories
- protect her from eating disorders and other cultural curses
- scare off the scoundrels and welcome the young men who might be worthy
- give your daughter a positive view of men

Jay will help you feel encouraged with 52 creative ideas to give you confidence in relating to your precious daughter...in ways that will help her blossom into the woman God has designed her to be.

365 Ways to Say "I Love You" to Your Kids

Expressions of love can get lost in the crush of carpools, diaper changes, homework, and afterschool activities. But Jay Payleitner is here to help you turn the dizzying array of activities into great memories. Learn to say "I love you"...

...at bedtime...in the car...in different languages... without words...doing chores...when your kids mess up big-time...on vacation...using secret phrases...in crazy unexpected ways...in everyday life...in ways that point to God.

Whether your kids are newborn or college-bound, these 365 simple suggestions—from silly to serious—will help you lead your precious pack to joy, laughter, and connection one "I love you" at a time.

52 Things Kids Need from a Dad
What Fathers Can Do to Make a Lifelong Difference

Good news—you are already the perfect dad for your kids! Still, you know you can grow. In the pages of this bestseller, Jay Payleitner, veteran radio producer and dad of five, offers a bounty of inspiring and unexpected insights:

- *straightforward rules*: "carry photos of your kids," "Dad tucks in," and "kiss your wife in the kitchen"
- *candid advice that may be tough to hear*: "get right with your own dad," "throw out your porn," and "surrender control of the TV remote"
- *weird topics that at first seem absurd*: "buy Peeps," "spin a bucket over your head" and "rent a dolphin"

Surely, God—our heavenly Father—designed fatherhood to be a joy, a blessing, and a blast! *A great gift or men's group resource.*

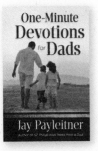

One-Minute Devotions for Dads

Lots of dads feel a twinge of terror at the word *devotion*. Something dull and guilt-producing. Something you're supposed to read at 5 a.m. before you do your 100 push-ups and eat your bowl of oat bran.

Enter Jay Payleitner, exit terror. A veteran dad, Jay knows how regular guys think because he is one. His Bible-based coaching sessions—devotions, if you must—offer you unexpected but relevant thoughts and touches of offbeat humor. And "What About You?" wrap-ups leave you with something straightforward to do or think about.

Young dads, older dads—your day will get a shot in the arm from Jay's seasoned wisdom and God-centered thinking.

OTHER HELPFUL RESOURCES
FROM HARVEST HOUSE

10 Ways to Prepare Your Son for Life
Steve Chapman

What Every Man Wishes His Father Had Told Him
Byron Yawn

8 Great Dates for Dads and Daughters
Talking with Your Daughter About Understanding Boys
Bob and Dannah Gresh

To learn more about Harvest House books and
to read sample chapters, visit our website:

www.harvesthousepublishers.com

HARVEST HOUSE PUBLISHERS
EUGENE, OREGON